Mathematics for
GCSE
and Standard Grade
Answer Book

David Rayner

Oxford University Press

Oxford University Press, Walton Street, Oxford OX2 6DP

Oxford New York Toronto
Delhi Bombay Calcutta Madras Karachi
Petaling Jaya Singapore Hong Kong Tokyo
Nairobi Dar es Salaam Cape Town
Melbourne Auckland

and associated companies in
Beirut Berlin

Oxford is a trade mark of Oxford University Press

© Oxford University Press 1987

ISBN 0 19 914274 2

First published 1987
Reprinted 1989, 1991

Printed in Hong Kong.
Typeset by Information Press Ltd.

Book 1

PART 1

Exercise 1   *page 1*

1. 58	**2.** 67	**3.** 251	**4.** 520	**5.** 961
6. 337	**7.** 496	**8.** 511	**9.** 320	**10.** 992
11. 647	**12.** 1071	**13.** 328	**14.** 940	**15.** 197
16. 2384	**17.** 3312	**18.** 5335	**19.** 7008	**20.** 8193
21. 1031	**22.** 3121	**23.** 3541	**24.** 827	**25.** 6890
26. 1021	**27.** 13 011	**28.** 21 844	**29.** 115 387	**30.** 19 885

Exercise 2   *page 1*

1. 34	**2.** 28	**3.** 23	**4.** 82	**5.** 111
6. 204	**7.** 57	**8.** 15	**9.** 56	**10.** 23
11. 137	**12.** 461	**13.** 381	**14.** 542	**15.** 301
16. 113	**17.** 533	**18.** 123	**19.** 522	**20.** 81
21. 265	**22.** 5646	**23.** 4819	**24.** 6388	**25.** 7832
26. 384	**27.** 399	**28.** 5804	**29.** 1361	**30.** 548
31. 355	**32.** 2325	**33.** 7130	**34.** 5071	**35.** 1734
36. 1499	**37.** 1879	**38.** 248	**39.** 3076	**40.** 573
41. 158	**42.** 397	**43.** 1797	**44.** 1416	**45.** 382
46. 9012	**47.** 47	**48.** 9360	**49.** 359	**50.** 16 333

Exercise 3   *page 2*

1.

3	8	1
2	4	6
7	0	5

2.

4	11	6
9	7	5
8	3	10

3.

8	1	6
3	5	7
4	9	2

4.

7	2	9
8	6	4
3	10	5

5.

12	7	14
13	11	9
8	15	10

6.

17	10	15
12	14	16
13	18	11

7.

1	12	7	14
8	13	2	11
10	3	16	5
15	6	9	4

8.

15	6	9	4
10	3	16	5
8	13	2	11
1	12	7	14

9.

3	10	12	17
14	15	5	8
9	4	18	11
16	13	7	6

10.

18	9	12	7
13	6	19	8
11	16	5	14
4	15	10	17

11.

11	24	7	20	3
4	12	25	8	16
17	5	13	21	9
10	18	1	14	22
23	6	19	2	15

12.

16	23	10	17	4
3	15	22	9	21
20	2	14	26	8
7	19	6	13	25
24	11	18	5	12

Exercise 4   page 3

1.

×	4	7	3	5	9	11	8	6	2	12
4	16	28	12	20	36	44	32	24	8	48
7	28	49	21	35	63	77	56	42	14	84
3	12	21	9	15	27	33	24	18	6	36
5	20	35	15	25	45	55	40	30	10	60
9	36	63	27	45	81	99	72	54	18	108
11	44	77	33	55	99	121	88	66	22	132
8	32	56	24	40	72	88	64	48	16	96
6	24	42	18	30	54	66	48	36	12	72
2	8	14	6	10	18	22	16	12	4	24
12	48	84	36	60	108	132	96	72	24	144

2.

×	7	5	9	6	8	11	4	2	12	3
7	49	35	63	42	56	77	28	14	84	21
5	35	25	45	30	40	55	20	10	60	15
9	63	45	81	54	72	99	36	18	108	27
6	42	30	54	36	48	66	24	12	72	18
8	56	40	72	48	64	88	32	16	96	24
11	77	55	99	66	88	121	44	22	132	33
4	28	20	36	24	32	44	16	8	48	12
2	14	10	18	12	16	22	8	4	24	6
12	84	60	108	72	96	132	48	24	144	36
3	21	15	27	18	24	33	12	6	36	9

Exercise 5   page 3

1. 63	**2.** 96	**3.** 252	**4.** 140	**5.** 639
6. 230	**7.** 1230	**8.** 168	**9.** 1477	**10.** 2114
11. 1065	**12.** 1923	**13.** 168	**14.** 1884	**15.** 1179
16. 1712	**17.** 4920	**18.** 3684	**19.** 12 846	**20.** 15 125
21. 2592	**22.** 4501	**23.** 2655	**24.** 6410	**25.** 8460
26. 2200	**27.** 4417	**28.** 7965	**29.** 3976	**30.** 12 918

Exercise 6   page 3

1. 345	**2.** 459	**3.** 943	**4.** 828	**5.** 1525
6. 1175	**7.** 4453	**8.** 3440	**9.** 464	**10.** 4853
11. 9744	**12.** 9021	**13.** 16 044	**14.** 31 772	**15.** 69 496
16. 65 832	**17.** 67 510	**18.** 143 676	**19.** 256 592	**20.** 734 266

Exercise 7   page 3

1. 23	**2.** 143	**3.** 211	**4.** 115	**5.** 178
6. 232	**7.** 527	**8.** 528	**9.** 83	**10.** 497
11. 273	**12.** 6024	**13.** 604	**14.** 271	**15.** 415
16. 383	**17.** 824	**18.** 936	**19.** 321	**20.** 2142
21. 9486	**22.** 2314	**23.** 241	**24.** 7005	**25.** 837
26. 6145	**27.** 2638	**28.** 415	**29.** 2060	**30.** 3104

Exercise 8   page 3

1. 325	**2.** 207	**3.** 418	**4.** 416	**5.** 6361
6. 635	**7.** 8089	**8.** 2497	**9.** 5627	**10.** 17 496
11. $535\frac{3}{4}$	**12.** $1283\frac{3}{5}$	**13.** $1506\frac{3}{4}$	**14.** $3440\frac{1}{7}$	**15.** $689\frac{1}{6}$
16. $130\frac{1}{3}$	**17.** $971\frac{1}{7}$	**18.** $2349\frac{1}{3}$	**19.** $254\frac{3}{8}$	**20.** $4420\frac{5}{6}$

Exercise 9   page 4

1. 14, 17	**2.** 21, 26	**3.** 12, 10	**4.** 30, 37	**5.** 26, 14
6. 16, 22	**7.** 19, 25	**8.** 40, 35	**9.** 22, 15	**10.** 80, 89
11. 64, 60	**12.** 4, 6	**13.** 7, 10	**14.** −10, −14	**15.** 23, 30
16. −4, −10	**17.** 4, 10	**18.** 51, 43	**19.** 96, 115	**20.** 25, 15

Exercise 10   page 4

1. 16, 32	**2.** 81, 243	**3.** 25, $12\frac{1}{2}$	**4.** 58, 67
5. 30 000, 300 000	**6.** 8, 4	**7.** 113, 120	**8.** 26, 20
9. I, K	**10.** N, Q	**11.** P, V	**12.** O, M
13. 155, $77\frac{1}{2}$	**14.** 25, 36	**15.** 120, 720	**16.** 5, 10
17. M, P	**18.** −11, −18	**19.** 26, 33	**20.** 43, 58
21. 3, 14	**22.** 2, $\frac{2}{3}$	**23.** 67, 47	**24.** $\frac{1}{3}, \frac{1}{9}$
25. 13, 21	**26.** M, R	**27.** 840, 6720	**28.** 22, 5
29. 32, 47	**30.** 17, 19		

Exercise 11   page 4

1. (c)	**2.** (c)	**3.** (b)	**4.** (a)	**5.** (b)	**6.** (c)
7. (c)	**8.** (c)	**9.** (a)	**10.** (c)	**11.** (c)	**12.** (c)
13. F	**14.** T	**15.** T	**16.** T	**17.** T	**18.** F
19. T	**20.** T	**21.** T	**22.** F	**23.** T	**24.** F
25. T	**26.** F	**27.** F	**28.** T	**29.** T	**30.** T
31. T	**32.** F	**33.** F	**34.** T	**35.** F	**36.** F
37. T	**38.** T	**39.** T	**40.** T		

Exercise 12   page 5

1. 0.12, 0.21, 0.31	**2.** 0.04, 0.35, 0.4	**3.** 0.67, 0.672, 0.7
4. 0.045, 0.05, 0.07	**5.** 0.089, 0.09, 0.1	**6.** 0.57, 0.705, 0.75
7. 0.041, 0.14, 0.41	**8.** 0.8, 0.809, 0.81	**9.** 0.006, 0.059, 0.6
10. 0.143, 0.15, 0.2	**11.** 0.04, 0.14, 0.2, 0.53	**12.** 0.12, 0.21, 1.12, 1.2
13. 0.08, 0.75, 2.03, 2.3	**14.** 0.26, 0.3, 0.602, 0.62	**15.** 0.5, 1.003, 1.03, 1.3
16. 0.709, 0.79, 0.792, 0.97	**17.** 0.312, 0.321, 1.04, 1.23	**18.** 0.0075, 0.008, 0.09, 0.091
19. 2, 2.046, 2.05, 2.5	**20.** 1.95, 5.1, 5.19, 9.51	**21.** 0.674, 0.706, 0.71, 0.76
22. 0.09, 0.989, 0.99, 1	**23.** 0.204, 0.24, 0.42, 1	**24.** 0.222, 0.3, 0.303, 0.33
25. 0.95, 1.02, 1.2, 1.21	**26.** 0.362, 0.632, 0.662, 3.62	**27.** 0.08, 0.096, 0.4, 1
28. 0.7, 0.72, 0.722, 0.732	**29.** 3.99, 4, 4.025, 4.03	**30.** 0.08, 0.658, 0.66, 0.685

Exercise 13   page 5

1. 10.14	**2.** 20.94	**3.** 26.71	**4.** 216.956	**5.** 9.6
6. 23.1	**7.** 12.25	**8.** 17.4	**9.** 0.0623	**10.** 85.47
11. 1.11	**12.** 4.36	**13.** 2.41	**14.** 10.8	**15.** 1.36
16. 6.23	**17.** 2.46	**18.** 12.24	**19.** 8.4	**20.** 15.96
21. 2.8	**22.** 2.2	**23.** 10.3	**24.** 21.8	**25.** 0.137
26. 0.0488	**27.** 6.65	**28.** 4.72	**29.** 0.566	**30.** 3.6

Exercise 14   page 5

1. 0.92	**2.** 1.08	**3.** 2.35	**4.** 8.52	**5.** 50
6. 2.982	**7.** 0.126	**8.** 0.302	**9.** 0.0692	**10.** 0.0504
11. 0.459	**12.** 0.002 52	**13.** 127.2	**14.** 10.86	**15.** 284.16
16. 0.0425	**17.** 0.0532	**18.** 3.6036	**19.** 0.000 218	**20.** 0.584
21. 2.99	**22.** 4.76	**23.** 7.815	**24.** 1.3062	**25.** 2.3488
26. 1.2465	**27.** 0.185 24	**28.** 21.164	**29.** 3.2852	**30.** 0.024 072

Exercise 15   page 6

1. 2.19	**2.** 9.87	**3.** 2.34	**4.** 2.31	**5.** 1.668
6. 3.45	**7.** 0.159	**8.** 0.313 75	**9.** 5.84	**10.** 2.652
11. 2.15	**12.** 0.35	**13.** 2.36	**14.** 8.59	**15.** 87.5
16. 0.184	**17.** 3.19	**18.** 2.13	**19.** 11.46	**20.** 3.64
21. 5.84	**22.** 36.1	**23.** 6.24	**24.** 0.548	**25.** 6.382
26. 0.259	**27.** 6.547	**28.** 104	**29.** 3575	**30.** 3287.5
31. 5.677	**32.** 6.238	**33.** 0.4963	**34.** 1400	**35.** 69.2
36. 4000	**37.** 0.5846	**38.** 0.002 59	**39.** 62.5	**40.** 2 734 000

Exercise 16   page 6

1. 6.34	**2.** 8.38	**3.** 81.5	**4.** 7.4	**5.** 7245
6. 61.05	**7.** 6.4	**8.** 7.5	**9.** 270	**10.** 35 100
11. 0.624	**12.** 0.897	**13.** 0.175	**14.** 0.0236	**15.** 0.048
16. 0.073	**17.** 0.127	**18.** 0.163	**19.** 58	**20.** 6.3
21. 75.1	**22.** 0.0084	**23.** 0.0111	**24.** 8.4	**25.** 16 000
26. 0.07	**27.** 0.008	**28.** 3170	**29.** 0.254	**30.** 99 000

Exercise 17   page 6

1. 4.32	**2.** 5.75	**3.** 9.16	**4.** 1.008	**5.** 0.748
6. 20.24	**7.** 10.2	**8.** 2.95	**9.** 4.926	**10.** 34
11. 0.621	**12.** 8.24	**13.** 0.1224	**14.** 12.15	**15.** 2.658
16. 66.462	**17.** 34 100	**18.** 0.0041	**19.** 2.104	**20.** 0.285
21. 0.258 84	**22.** 3.27	**23.** 2.247	**24.** 0.54	**25.** 0.027
26. 6.6077	**27.** 6.56	**28.** 7.84	**29.** 0.005 84	**30.** 742 000

Exercise 18   page 7

1. 0.103	**2.** 6.25	**3.** 12.1	**4.** 3.4	**5.** 620
6. 8.26	**7.** 41.42	**8.** 1.605	**9.** 0.009	**10.** 0.34
11. 26 000	**12.** 0.009 624	**13.** 47.8	**14.** 0.3113	**15.** 65.14
16. 5.68	**17.** 3.402	**18.** 9.8	**19.** 8.47	**20.** 177.5
21. 0.8925	**22.** 40 000	**23.** 2.331	**24.** 25.8	**25.** 0.0082
26. 6.548	**27.** 131.8	**28.** 19.98	**29.** 63.49	**30.** 520

Exercise 19   *page 7*

1. 75%	**2.** 40%	**3.** 50%	**4.** 80%	**5.** 25%
6. $62\frac{1}{2}$%	**7.** 90%	**8.** 85%	**9.** 25%	**10.** $87\frac{1}{2}$%
11. 68%	**12.** 35%	**13.** 7%	**14.** $33\frac{1}{3}$%	**15.** $66\frac{2}{3}$%
16. $12\frac{1}{2}$%	**17.** 98%	**18.** 25%	**19.** 61%	**20.** 25%
21. 32%	**22.** $67\frac{1}{2}$%	**23.** $33\frac{1}{3}$%	**24.** $23\frac{1}{2}$%	**25.** 68%
26. 90%	**27.** 65%	**28.** 40%	**29.** $22\frac{1}{2}$%	**30.** 34%
31. 98%	**32.** 25%	**33.** $47\frac{1}{2}$%	**34.** $33\frac{1}{3}$%	**35.** 6.7%

Exercise 20   *page 7*

1. (a) 44%   (b) 65%   **2.** 21%   **3.** (a) 50%   (b) 40%   (c) 10%
4. (a) 25   (b) 44%   (c) 56%   **5.** Susan 70%, Jane 54%, Jackie 52%
6. 54%   **7.** (a) 48%   (b) 76%   **8.** 4%
9. (a) $37\frac{1}{2}$%   (b) $12\frac{1}{2}$%   (c) 0%   (d) $37\frac{1}{2}$%   **10.** 40%

Exercise 21   *page 8*

1. £12	**2.** £8	**3.** £10	**4.** £3	**5.** £2.40
6. £24	**7.** £45	**8.** £72	**9.** £244	**10.** £9.60
11. $42	**12.** $88	**13.** 8 kg	**14.** 12 kg	**15.** 272 g
16. 45 m	**17.** 40 km	**18.** $710	**19.** 4.94 kg	**20.** 60 g
21. £1340	**22.** 245 kg	**23.** £96.80	**24.** £95.20	**25.** £22.10
26. £70.08	**27.** £66	**28.** £112.50	**29.** £112	**30.** £169.65

Exercise 22   *page 8*

1. £0.28	**2.** £1.16	**3.** £1.22	**4.** £2.90	**5.** £3.57
6. £0.45	**7.** £0.93	**8.** £37.03	**9.** £16.97	**10.** £0.38
11. £0.79	**12.** £1.60	**13.** £13.40	**14.** £50	**15.** £2.94
16. £11.06	**17.** £1.23	**18.** £4.40	**19.** £11.25	**20.** £22.71
21. £0.12	**22.** £0.03	**23.** £1.11	**24.** £93.50	**25.** £95.94
26. £426.87	**27.** £0.04 ×	**28.** £0.13	**29.** £6.80	**30.** £0.88

Exercise 23   *page 9*

1. £13.20	**2.** £42	**3.** £69	**4.** £87.36	**5.** £84
6. £46	**7.** £45	**8.** £60.80	**9.** £7.56	**10.** £8.91
11. £63	**12.** £736	**13.** £77.55	**14.** £104	**15.** £1960
16. £792	**17.** £132	**18.** £45.75	**19.** £110.30	**20.** £42
21. £12.03	**22.** £9.49	**23.** £7.35	**24.** £7.01	**25.** £12.34
26. £16.92	**27.** £31.87	**28.** £9.02	**29.** £8.88	**30.** £14.14

Exercise 24   *page 9*

1. £35.20	**2.** £5724	**3.** £171.50	**4.** £88.35	**5.** 2.828 kg
6. £58.50	**7.** 24	**8.** 59 400	**9.** £9.52	**10.** 3.348 kg
11. 13.054 kg	**12.** £2762.50			

13. (b) £43.70   (c) £48.30   (d) £243.80   (e) £9.43
14. (a) £25.20   (b) £33.25   (c) £46.75   (d) £156   (e) £7.98

Exercise 25   *page 10*

1. £17.14   **2.** £39.79   **3.** £76.30   **4.** £181.40
5. (a) £28   (b) £21   **6.** (a) £51   (b) £40.80   **7.** £396
8. (a) £480   (b) (i) £16.20   (ii) £1053

Exercise 26   *page 10*

1. (a) £40   (b) £36   (c) £80   **2.** £28, £15.75, 10% , £37.20, 20%
3. (a) £5000   (b) £1000   (c) £4000, £3200, £2560
4. (a) £45   (b) £495   (c) £41.25   **5.** 40% , 35%, 10%, 5%
6. (a) 40p   (b) £25   (c) £5   **7.** 4200 kg   **8.** (a) £5000   (b) 16.7%

Exercise 27   *page 11*

1. £10, £20   **2.** £45, £15   **3.** £12, £8   **4.** £7, £35
5. 330 g, 550 g   **6.** $480, $600   **7.** 36, 90   **8.** £10, £20, £30
9. £100, £150, £150   **10.** £12, £36, £48   **11.** $1200, $1800, $2400   **12.** 52, 78, 130
13. 160 g, 320 g, 400 g **14.** £70   **15.** £50   **16.** £137.50
17. 40 g   **18.** 3250   **19.** 45p   **20.** £24.40

Exercise 28   *page 12*

1. $9, $18, $13.50, $4.50   **2.** £66, £44, £110, £110
3. 600 kg, 1500 kg, 300 kg, 1800 kg   **4.** 224 g
5. £9.10   **6.** £16
7. £166.50   **8.** £64, £32
9. £30, £90   **10.** £48, £24, £12
11. £360, £180, £60   **12.** £72, £144, £36
13. A £50,   B £200,   C £100   **14.** A £96,   B £24,   C £48
15. A £6,   B £36,   C £12

Exercise 29   *page 12*

1. 8   **2.** 5   **3.** 9   **4.** £100
5. £42   **6.** 30 g zinc, 40 g tin   **7.** 24   **8.** 36
9. 16 white, 8 green   **10.** 16 horses, 128 cows

Exercise 30   *page 13*

1. £24   **2.** £1.08   **3.** £3.15   **4.** £5.88
5. £1.26, £4.20   **6.** £2.20, £22   **7.** £97.50   **8.** 2750 g
9. 1400   **10.** 4.5 litres   **11.** £3.45   **12.** £1.61
13. £3.99   **14.** 125 s   **15.** 90 min

Exercise 31   *page 13*

1. 10   **2.** 10   **3.** 12   **4.** 20, 35
5. 100   **6.** 160   **7.** 450   **8.** 267, 11
9. £12.75, 20   **10.** £2.24, £4.20   **11.** £1.60, £3.60   **12.** 35 litres
13. 200 litres   **14.** 70 gallons

Exercise 32   *page 14*

1. 18 h   **2.** 3 h   **3.** 6 days   **4.** 6 h
5. 8 days, $\frac{1}{2}$ day   **6.** 40 h   **7.** 24 days   **8.** 4 days
9. 24   **10.** 8   **11.** 12, 3, 4, $1\frac{1}{2}$ **12.** 80, 24, 1000, $1\frac{1}{2}$
13. 1500, 3000, 1, 120   **14.** 30   **15.** 120 min., 40 min.   **16.** 30 min., 360 min.

PART 2

Exercise 1   *page 15*

1. 7.24	**2.** 4.1	**3.** 162.5	**4.** 23.1	**5.** 800
6. 170	**7.** 6000	**8.** 60	**9.** 200	**10.** 1300
11. 110	**12.** 4	**13.** 3200	**14.** 1560	**15.** 7000
16. 700	**17.** 0.7	**18.** 0.2	**19.** 74	**20.** 6230
21. 8.24	**22.** 7.96	**23.** 0.973	**24.** 1.112	**25.** 2.7
26. 3.73	**27.** 0.242	**28.** 0.082	**29.** 0.06	**30.** 0.11
31. 0.004	**32.** 0.002	**33.** 0.0023	**34.** 0.01	**35.** 0.182
36. 0.079	**37.** 0.02	**38.** 0.0071	**39.** 0.013	**40.** 0.084
41. 230	**42.** 0.82	**43.** 410	**44.** 1700	**45.** 1.7
46. 0.06	**47.** 8970	**48.** 1100	**49.** 0.08	**50.** 6
51. 2000	**52.** 18 000			

Exercise 2   *page 16*

1. 127 cm	**2.** 65 cm	**3.** 300 cm	**4.** 7 cm	**5.** 1100 cm
6. 810 cm	**7.** 234 cm	**8.** 0.2 cm	**9.** 0.17 m	**10.** 0.24 m
11. 2.4 m	**12.** 0.11 m	**13.** 0.02 m	**14.** 0.182 m	**15.** 0.031 m
16. 50 m	**17.** 630 cm	**18.** 24 cm	**19.** 0.67 m	**20.** 0.09 m
21. 1.7 cm	**22.** 2.5 cm	**23.** 25 cm	**24.** 1.2 cm	**25.** 20 mm
26. 150 mm	**27.** 28 mm	**28.** 96 mm	**29.** 2000 m	**30.** 1500 m
31. 1240 m	**32.** 324 m	**33.** 76 m	**34.** 18 000 m	**35.** 7100 m
36. 70 m	**37.** 0.4 km	**38.** 0.875 km	**39.** 2.5 cm	**40.** 0.065 km
41. 0.45 kg	**42.** 0.2 kg	**43.** 1.4 kg	**44.** 2.65 kg	**45.** 0.04 kg
46. 0.055 kg	**47.** 0.007 kg	**48.** 7 kg	**49.** 2200 g	**50.** 650 g
51. 2000 kg	**52.** 3200 kg	**53.** 0.5 l	**54.** 4 m^3	**55.** 6 m^3
56. 8 l	**57.** 0.455 l	**58.** 2450 ml	**59.** 2800 kg	**60.** 0.067 kg

Exercise 3   *page 16*

1. 0.32 cm	**2.** 1.5 cm	**3.** 0.234 kg	**4.** 0.072 km	**5.** 750 cm
6. 41 g	**7.** 0.26 l	**8.** 7.1 mm	**9.** 0.09 m	**10.** 100 000 m
11. 0.027 kg	**12.** 0.7 cm	**13.** 18 000 g	**14.** 0.8 l	**15.** 200 m
16. 1110 cm	**17.** 0.4 t	**18.** 1 000 000 g	**19.** 0.085 km	**20.** 0.03 cm
21. 0.08 m	**22.** 0.006 kg	**23.** 10 cm	**24.** 0.95 l	**25.** 7800 kg
26. 70 g	**27.** 0.2 m	**28.** 600 cm	**29.** 0.018 kg	**30.** 0.88 km
31. 0.07 km	**32.** 0.6 m	**33.** 30 mm	**34.** 710 m	**35.** 0.02 t
36. 0.05 m^3	**37.** 0.006 km	**38.** 0.017 kg	**39.** 25 000 cm	**40.** 0.0001 m

Exercise 4   *page 16*

1. 24.3 cm   **2.** £2.52   **3.** 73   **4.** 23   **5.** 2576
6. £17.70   **7.** 0.6 kg   **8.** (a) 34, 25   (b) 15, 7.5   (c) 12, 17   (d) 44, 32
9. £5   **10.** (a) What time do we finish.   (b) Spurs are rubbish.   (c) We are under attack.

Exercise 5   *page 17*

1. 582	**2.** £5.12	**3.** 130 years	**4.** £28.50	**5.** 14 55
6. 15 h 5 min	**7.** £10.35	**8.** £21.10	**9.** 3854	**10.** £704

Exercise 6   *page 17*

1. 21	**2.** 50 kg	**3.** 91p	**4.** $1\frac{1}{2}$	**5.** $\frac{2}{3}$
6. 6p	**7.** 16p	**8.** 24	**9.** 24	**10.** Both same (!)

Exercise 7   *page 18*

1. £3.26   **2.** £1.70   **3.** 8   **4.** 215   **5.** 100 m
6. £184.50   **7.** £839.50   **8.** £2
9. (a) $99 + \frac{9}{9}$ (b) $6 + \frac{6}{6}$ (c) $55 + 5$ (d) $55 + 5 + \frac{5}{5}$ (e) $\frac{7+7}{7+7}$ (f) $\frac{88}{8}$
10. From left to right: (a) 7, 3   (b) 4, 3   (c) 7, 8, 6   (d) 3, 7, 0   (e) 3, 6   (f) 6, 8, 0

Exercise 8   *page 18*

1. £62   **2.** £570   **3.** 9 h 15 min   **4.** 10. 26 m^2, 1.74 m^2 **5.** 86 400
6. (a) 14, 17   (b) 17, 22   (c) 2, −3   (d) 63, 127   **7.** £37.80   **8.** £1 = F12.1
9. (a) 39, 38, 38, 36, 35, 31, 30, 28   (b) 27, 27, 26, 26, 24, 22, 20, 20   **10.** £5.85

Exercise 9   *page 19*

1. 5p   **2.** 0.012, 0.021, 0.03, 0.12, 0.21   **3.** 51.4°   4. Jars by 24p   **5.** 4.5 litres
6. 2.05 m, 1.95 m   **7.** (a) £66   (b) £720   (c) £2040   **8.** £24
9. 9, 8, 25, 1000, 32, 48   **10.** 6p, 30p, 21p

Exercise 10   *page 19*

1. 9   **2.** 5 m, 50 m, 6 km   **3.** £2.50
4. (a) 3, 4   (b) 7, 6   (c) 8, 4   (d) 24, 2
5. (b) 0.25   (c) $\frac{3}{10}$ (d) 0.125   (e) $\frac{1}{20}$ (f) 0.001
6. (a) £800   (b) 8%   **7.** 10 h 30 min
8. (a) 0.54   (b) 40   (c) 0.004   (d) 2.2   (e) £9   (f) £40
9. 260 million   **10.** (a) 1050 g   (b) 3

Exercise 11   *page 20*

1. 22   **2.** 19.35   **3.** 120°   **4.** £22.40
5. 2333, 3102, 3120, 3210, 3211, 3301
6. (a) 270   (b) 4100   (c) 0.0084   (d) 5.23
7. 18 000   **8.** 18   **9.** 1296, 322
10. (a) yes   (b) no   (c) yes   (d) yes   (e) yes   (f) yes   (g) yes   (h) no

Exercise 12   *page 21*

1. (a) £136   (b) £30.60   (c) £142.05   **2.** 25 cm^2
3. (a) £2.15   (b) £2.45   (c) £2.93   **4.** 44 cm
5. (a) £523   (b) £624   (c) £366.10   **6.** 16   **8.** 64 mph
9. (a) 69   (l) 65   **10.** 4p

Exercise 13   *page 22*

1. (a) £64   (b) £124   (c) 100 km
2. (a) £106, £161, £126, £119   (b) £47   (c) £665   (d) £380
4. (a) £16.50   (b) £20   **5.** (a) 59 040   (b) 21 608 640   (c) £4 321 728

Exercise 14   *page 23*

1. 24   **2.** 9   **3.** 32   **4.** 16   **5.** 42   **6.** 60
7. 17 600   **8.** 80   **9.** 4480   **10.** 36   **11.** 140   **12.** 224
13. 18   **14.** 8   **15.** 440   **16.** 360   **17.** 4   **18.** 2
19. 56   **20.** 16   **21.** 72   **22.** 3520   **23.** 5   **24.** 2
25. 2   **26.** 48   **27.** 108   **28.** 18   **29.** 880   **30.** 4
31. 54   **32.** 54   **33.** 72   **34.** 102   **35.** 152   **36.** 63
37. 73   **38.** 58

Exercise 15   *page 23*

1. 25.4	**2.** 45.5	**3.** 45.4	**4.** 56.8	**5.** 3.22	**6.** 0.908
7. 16.1	**8.** 10.16	**9.** 2.27	**10.** 0.284	**11.** 6.21	**12.** 22
13. 6.6	**14.** 62.1	**15.** 88	**16.** 4.4	**17.** 1.242	**18.** 1.1
19. 44	**20.** 12.42	**21.** 30.48	**22.** 2.84	**23.** 0.66	**24.** 7.62
25. 1.816					

Exercise 16   *page 24*

1. F120	**2.** DM80	**3.** DR450	**4.** Ptas20 000	**5.** $1400
6. DR1200	**7.** F84	**8.** $140	**9.** DM64	**10.** DM2000
11. F6	**12.** Ptas100	**13.** $0.70	**14.** DR150 000	**15.** Ptas200 000
16. DM1	**17.** F3	**18.** $70	**19.** DR30 000	**20.** Ptas20
21. $700	**22.** F7200	**23.** DM260	**24.** DR4500	**25.** F18
26. $1.40	**27.** DR225	**28.** Ptas500	**29.** Ptas2200	**30.** $17.50

Exercise 17   *page 24*

1. £3	**2.** £10	**3.** £2	**4.** £5	**5.** £4
6. £10	**7.** £100	**8.** £20	**9.** £25	**10.** £10
11. £8	**12.** £50	**13.** £1.50	**14.** £4.50	**15.** £0.53
16. £5.42	**17.** £42.86	**18.** £20.50	**19.** £8.75	**20.** £32.50
21. £15.50	**22.** £642.86	**23.** £0.47	**24.** £20	**25.** £50
26. £0.63	**27.** £16.07	**28.** £4.83	**29.** £22.10	**30.** £6.05
31. £42.50	**32.** £50.71	**33.** £4.27	**34.** £1.27	**35.** £542.86
36. £79.25	**37.** £4750	**38.** £3000	**39.** £1875	**40.** £182.14

Exercise 18   *page 24*

1. F240	**2.** DM60	**3.** £10	**4.** £3	**5.** Ptas1000
6. £9	**7.** £15	**8.** $428.57	**9.** £2.25	**10.** £21
11. £3.93	**12.** £3333.33	**13.** DR48 000	**14.** £0.93	**15.** Germany £25
16. France £240	**17.** U.S.A. £0.50	**18.** (a) £100	(b) F1200	(c) F1200

Exercise 19   *page 25*

1. 200 m	**2.** 500 m	**3.** (a) 2 km	(b) 3 km	(c) 0.8 km		
4. (a) 5 km	(b) 3 km	(c) 6 km				
5. (b) 200 m	(c) 1 km	(d) 0.6 km	(e) 1.5 km	(f) 2.5 km	(g) 2.2 km	
(h) 2 km	(i) 1.55 km	(j) 270 m				
6. 1.08 km	**7.** 63 m	**8.** 24 km	**9.** 19.52 km	**10.** 5.888 km	**11.** 120 m	
12. 5.6 m	**13.** 5 m	**14.** 90 m	**15.** 10.5 m			

Exercise 20   *page 26*

1. 150 cm	**2.** 125 cm	**3.** 28 cm	**4.** 5.9 cm		
5. (a) 60 cm	(b) 84 cm	(c) 56 cm	(d) 140 cm	(e) 100 cm	(f) 6 cm
(g) 50 cm	(h) 220 cm	(i) 0.6 cm	**6.** 13 cm	**7.** 2.5 cm	**8.** 1.5 cm

Exercise 21   *page 26*

1. 4.4 km	**2.** 250 cm				
3. (a) 0.5 km	(b) 120 cm	(c) 1.68 km	(d) 16 cm	(e) 6.4 km	(f) 0.2 cm
(g) 3 m	(h) 1.54 km	(i) 1: 10 000	(j) 1: 20 000	(k) 1: 100 000	(l) 1: 20 000
(m) 1: 50 000					
4. 1: 10 000	**5.** 1: 20 000	**6.** 1: 50 000	**7.** 7.3 m, 3.5 m, 2.5 m		

PART 3

Exercise 1   *page 27*

1. 3.18	**2.** 14.8	**3.** 8.05	**4.** 2.63	**5.** 51.3
6. 0.557	**7.** 0.832	**8.** 7.37	**9.** 0.0761	**10.** 18.3
11. 427	**12.** 315	**13.** 6.01	**14.** 11.4	**15.** 2.09
16. 0.007 42	**17.** 318	**18.** 2420	**19.** 3560	**20.** 38 700
21. 5.7	**22.** 18	**23.** 0.77	**24.** 0.52	**25.** 8.3
26. 7.2	**27.** 12	**28.** 25	**29.** 19	**30.** 0.0083
31. 0.071	**32.** 18	**33.** 31	**34.** 61	**35.** 19 000
36. 34 000	**37.** 890	**38.** 72 000	**39.** 40 000	**40.** 160
41. 28.67	**42.** 3.041	**43.** 2.995	**44.** 316.3	**45.** 8.046
46. 0.007 165	**47.** 0.031 11	**48.** 84 210	**49.** 65 530	**50.** 124 900
51. 5.678	**52.** 193.2	**53.** 568.8	**54.** 2002	**55.** 0.038 11
56. 76.06	**57.** 80.05	**58.** 6.067	**59.** 77 780	**60.** 400 300

Exercise 2   *page 28*

1. 8.49	**2.** 6.04	**3.** 1.04	**4.** 12.14	**5.** 11.62
6. 6.05	**7.** 0.56	**8.** 18.08	**9.** 2.05	**10.** 8.95
11. 13.62	**12.** 216.84	**13.** 0.07	**14.** 0.07	**15.** 7.82
16. 3.13	**17.** 4.11	**18.** 24.52	**19.** 206.13	**20.** 8.09
21. 8.6	**22.** 12.6	**23.** 9.0	**24.** 2.6	**25.** 8.6
26. 5.7	**27.** 0.7	**28.** 0.1	**29.** 8.8	**30.** 0.7
31. 207.2	**32.** 10.7	**33.** 0.1	**34.** 8.0	**35.** 4.3
36. 88.7	**37.** 217.1	**38.** 4.0	**39.** 0.9	**40.** 5.0
41. 8.05	**42.** 17.6	**43.** 6.8	**44.** 9.09	**45.** 0.071
46. 0.0333	**47.** 19.6	**48.** 8.076	**49.** 8.09	**50.** 4.08
51. 3.336	**52.** 8.9	**53.** 8.05	**54.** 0.08	**55.** 0.0715
56. 2.3	**57.** 8.072	**58.** 1.350	**59.** 9.9	**60.** 16.0

61. (a) 5.8 cm by 3.6 cm, 5.1 cm by 3.6 cm   (b) 20.9 cm^2, 18.4 cm^2

Exercise 3   *page 29*

1. C	**2.** A	**3.** B	**4.** B	**5.** C	**6.** A	**7.** B
8. B	**9.** A	**10.** C	**11.** C	**12.** A	**13.** B	**14.** A
15. C	**16.** B	**17.** C	**18.** A	**19.** B	**20.** B	**21.** C
22. A	**23.** B	**24.** C	**25.** A	**26.** B	**27.** C	**28.** B
29. C	**30.** B					

Exercise 4   *page 30*

1. B	**2.** A	**3.** C	**4.** A	**5.** B	**6.** C	**7.** A
8. B	**9.** A	**10.** C	**11.** B	**12.** A	**13.** C	**14.** A
15. B	**16.** A	**17.** B	**18.** C	**19.** B	**20.** B	**21.** A
22. C	**23.** C	**24.** B	**25.** C	**26.** A	**27.** B	**28.** B
29. C	**30.** B					

Exercise 5   *page 30*

1. 20	**2.** 13	**3.** 16	**4.** 22	**5.** 4	**6.** 13	**7.** 12
8. 10	**9.** 5	**10.** 15	**11.** 20	**12.** 6	**13.** 5	**14.** 47
15. 30	**16.** 22	**17.** 18	**18.** 15	**19.** 1	**20.** 23	**21.** 19
22. 4	**23.** 3	**24.** 0	**25.** 35	**26.** 60	**27.** 16	**28.** 6
29. 13	**30.** 14	**31.** 23	**32.** 71	**33.** 20	**34.** 36	**35.** 9
36. 8	**37.** 32	**38.** 30	**39.** 4	**40.** 0	**41.** 37	**42.** 46

43. 0 **44.** 35 **45.** 74 **46.** 1 **47.** 5 **48.** 7 **49.** 6
50. 20 **51.** 7 **52.** 95 **53.** 14 **54.** 7 **55.** 20 **56.** 89
57. 50 **58.** 8 **59.** 5 **60.** 366

Exercise 6   *page 31*

1. 13 **2.** 15 **3.** 23 **4.** 27 **5.** 15 **6.** 28 **7.** 97
8. 17 **9.** 7 **10.** 5 **11.** 22 **12.** 16 **13.** 20 **14.** 5
15. 13 **16.** 58 **17.** 29 **18.** 80 **19.** 9 **20.** 10 **21.** 20
22. 34 **23.** 18 **24.** 5 **25.** 44 **26.** 28 **27.** 13 **28.** 32
29. 5 **30.** 21 **31.** 17 **32.** 36 **33.** 39 **34.** 80 **35.** 51
36. 1 **37.** 5 **38.** 54 **39.** 14 **40.** 78 **41.** 51 **42.** 14
43. 97 **44.** 4 **45.** 24 **46.** 41 **47.** 23 **48.** 17 **49.** 23
50. 11 **51.** 5 **52.** 6 **53.** 4 **54.** 4 **55.** 6 **56.** 5
57. 1 **58.** 47 **59.** 6 **60.** 3 **61.** 16 **62.** 12 **63.** 52
64. 15 **65.** 87 **66.** 17 **67.** 23 **68.** 8 **69.** 2 **70.** 26

Exercise 7   *page 32*

1. 1851 **2.** 6.889 **3.** 1.214 **4.** 0.4189 **5.** 7.889
6. 19.35 **7.** 0.049 47 **8.** 221.5 **9.** 24.37 **10.** 6.619
11. 3.306 **12.** 2.303 **13.** 41.73 **14.** 8.163 **15.** 0.1090
16. 0.5001 **17.** 20.63 **18.** 10.09 **19.** 6.191 **20.** 10.27
21. 8.627 **22.** 22.02 **23.** 1.093 **24.** 44.72 **25.** 45.66
26. 52.86 **27.** 22.51 **28.** 5.479 **29.** 5.272 **30.** 0.2116
31. 4.605 **32.** 1.153

Exercise 8   *page 32*

1. 14.52 **2.** 1.666 **3.** 1.858 **4.** 0.8264 **5.** 2.717
6. 4.840 **7.** 10.87 **8.** 7.425 **9.** 13.49 **10.** 0.7392
11. 1135 **12.** 13.33 **13.** 5.836 **14.** 86.39 **15.** 10.23
16. 5540 **17.** 14.76 **18.** 8.502 **19.** 57.19 **20.** 19.90
21. 6.578 **22.** 9.907 **23.** 0.082 80 **24.** 1855 **25.** 2.367
26. 1.416 **27.** 7.261 **28.** 3.151 **29.** 149.9 **30.** 74 020
31. 8.482 **32.** 75.21 **33.** 1.226 **34.** 6767 **35.** 5.964
36. 15.45 **37.** 25.42 **38.** 2.724 **39.** 4.366 **40.** 0.2194

Exercise 9   *page 33*

1. 5.6×10^5 **2.** 2.44×10^8 **3.** 7.2×10^4 **4.** 1.31×10^5
5. 8.5×10^7 **6.** 9×10^8 **7.** 7.34×10^{10} **8.** 8.42×10^9
9. 6.6×10^4 **10.** 2×10^{12} **11.** 1×10^8 **12.** 2×10^9
13. 4.4×10^2 **14.** 6×10^4 **15.** 1.6×10^5 **16.** 4.85×10^9
17. 1.8472×10^4 **18.** $6.358\ 11 \times 10^5$ **19.** $3.333\ 333 \times 10^6$ **20.** $8.211\ 111 \times 10^6$
21. 4×10^{-6} **22.** 5.2×10^{-6} **23.** 7.411×10^{-6} **24.** 4.32×10^{-3}
25. 7.5×10^{-3} **26.** 8.239×10^{-3} **27.** 7×10^{-9} **28.** 1.5×10^{-8}
29. 2×10^{-10} **30.** 4.6×10^{-3} **31.** 7.4×10^{-3} **32.** 6.31×10^{-3}
33. 8.4×10^4 **34.** 1.2×10^7 **35.** 2×10^{-6} **36.** 4.53×10^{-8}
37. 1.6×10^{10} **38.** 7.24×10^{-1} **39.** $2.844\ 44 \times 10^5$ **40.** 2.22×10^{-6}
41. 3.2×10^6 **42.** 6×10^9 **43.** 1.82×10^6 **44.** 4×10^{-7}
45. 7×10^{-7} **46.** 7×10^{-8} **47.** 6.66×10^{10} **48.** 7.1×10^{11}
49. 3.2×10^{-8} **50.** 1.62×10^{-6}

Exercise 10   *page 33*

1. 360 000 **2.** 72 200 000 **3.** 82 000 **4.** 6 000 000
5. 1 100 000 000 **6.** 324 000 **7.** 100 000 000 000 **8.** 6 360 000

9. 8 020 000 000   10. 32 000   11. 670   12. 30 300
13. 89 900 000   14. 10 200 000 000   15. 6 200 000   16. 0.000 26
17. 0.081   18. 0.000 01   19. 0.000 003   20. 0.000 000 44
21. 0.008   22. 0.000 000 12   23. 0.000 000 095   24. 0.000 000 000 046
25. 88 000   26. 2750   27. 0.001 01   28. 0.000 009 6
29. 0.000 07   30. 320

Exercise 11   *page 33*

1. 10^7 2. 10^9 3. 10^{10} 4. 10^5 5. 10^6 6. 10^2 7. 10^{-7}
8. 10^{-2} 9. 10^{-8} 10. 10^{-5} 11. 10^{-8} 12. 10^2 13. 10^4 14. 10^5
15. 10^8 16. 10^{-4} 17. 10^{-13} 18. 10^6 19. 10^8 20. 10^{11} 21. 10^{-8}
22. 10^7 23. 10^{-3} 24. 10^8

Exercise 12   *page 33*

1. 6×10^9 2. 3×10^{13} 3. 6.6×10^{17} 4. 8.8×10^{13} 5. 8×10^4
6. 8.5×10^9 7. 6.9×10^{-6} 8. 7×10^5 9. 6.28×10^{16} 10. 7.2×10^{-4}
11. 4.4×10^6 12. 4.5×10^3 13. 1.5×10^6 14. 8×10^3 15. 3×10^{-5}
16. 2×10^{-6} 17. 3.6×10^{-6} 18. 1.7×10^6 19. 3×10^9 20. 3.1×10^7

THINK ABOUT IT   1

Exercise A   *page 35*

1. 23 and 2 over   2. 42   3. 2675   4. £9.20   5. 6
6. 6, 4   7. 6 km   8. 740   9. $5\frac{1}{2}$ h   10. 3

Exercise B   *page 36*

1. 273 377   2. 120°, 30°   3. 845   4. £58.05   5. 61   6. 1000, 96
7. £274   8. 4400, £2.50   9. $x = 203.13$, $y = 777.21$, $z = 585.71$ 10. £26.25

Exercise C   *page 38*

3. Man. Utd   19 points
   Liverpool   19 points
   Everton   18 points
   Arsenal   10 points
   Notts Forest   9 points
   West Ham   7 points

4. £115 625   5. £113 808   6. £479 770   7. £11 034

Exercise D   *page 41*

1. 2.3 kg   2. (a) 2 m   (b) 230 cm   (c) 7200 m   (d) 80 cm   (e) 0.028 km   (f) 2.5 cm
3. £1320   5. 50, $\frac{3}{4}$ 6. £19   7. £53 250   8. £1860   9. 12
10. (a) 100 cm^2 (b) 3 cm   (c) 30 cm^2

Project 5   *page 42*

triangle, fraction, decimal, degree, ruler, seven, total, area, volume, two, add, one, ten, centimetre, pencil, dozen, foot, inch, gram, even.

Exercise E   *page 43*

1. 480 g   **2.** (c) 5 cm^2 **3.** (a) 70 m   (b) 700 m   (c) 42 km
4. £17, 8.4 kg   **5.** 50p   **6.** 5% of £80 = £4
7. (a) 5   (b) 30   (c) 12   (d) 100   (e) 9   (f) 0.1
8. (a) $\frac{1}{5}$ (b) $\frac{3}{4}$ (c) 50%   (d) $\frac{9}{10}$ (e) 25%   (f) $\frac{1}{10}$
9. 30, $\frac{1}{3}$ **10.** £8.75

Exercise F   *page 45*

1. 0.03, 0.058, 0.07, 0.085, 0.11   **2.** (a) £270   (b) £4050   (c) £4.05   **3.** 13
4. (a) 17, 21   (b) 37, 46   (c) 3, $1\frac{1}{2}$ (d) 25, 36   **5.** 69   **6.** $7\frac{1}{2}$
7. (a) $\frac{3}{4}$ (b) $\frac{2}{3}$ (c) $\frac{5}{8}$ (d) $\frac{2}{5}$
8. 0.5, 50%; $\frac{1}{5}$, 20%; $\frac{1}{10}$, 0.1; 0.375, $37\frac{1}{2}$%; $\frac{9}{10}$, 0.9
9. £3750, £33 750   **10.** (a) 260 km   (b) 26 litres   (c) £11.05

Exercise G   *page 46*

1. 15, 17   **2.** 10, 7   **3.** 36, 43   **4.** 17, 23   **5.** 41, 36
6. 16, 32   **7.** 29, 20   **8.** 6, 3   **9.** 120, 720   **10.** 10, 13
11. 13, 12   **12.** 39, 65   **13.** 25, 36   **14.** 18, $4\frac{1}{2}$ **15.** $\frac{1}{4}$, $\frac{1}{16}$
16. 7, 9   **17.** 240, 1440   **18.** 30, 15   **19.** 8, 216   **20.** 82, 100

21. (a) $6 \times 7 = 6 + 6^2$ (b) $10 \times 11 = 10 + 10^2$
          $7 \times 8 = 7 + 7^2$ $30 \times 31 = 30 + 30^2$

22. (a) $7^2 = 5^2 + 4 \times 5 + 4$ (b) $12^2 = 10^2 + 4 \times 10 + 4$
          $8^2 = 6^2 + 4 \times 6 + 4$ $22^2 = 20^2 + 4 \times 20 + 4$

23. (a) $5^2 = 1 + 3 + 5 + 7 + 9$ (b) $10^2 = 1 + 3 + 5 + ... + 19$
          $6^2 = 1 + 3 + 5 + 7 + 9 + 11$ $15^2 = 1 + 3 + 5 + ... + 29$

PART 4

Exercise 1   *page 50*

1. 24 cm^2 **2.** 14 cm^2 **3.** 144 cm^2 **4.** 15 cm^2 **5.** 33 cm^2 **6.** 75 mm^2 **7.** 25 ~~m^2~~ c m^2
8. 12 cm^2 **9.** 153 cm^2 **10.** 20 m^2 **11.** 42 cm^2 **12.** $7\frac{1}{2}$ cm^2 **13.** 20 km^2 **14.** 24 mm^2

Exercise 2   *page 51*

1. 36 cm^2 **2.** 77 m^2 **3.** 96 cm^2 **4.** 36 m^2 **5.** 54 m^2 **6.** 25 m^2 **7.** 28 m^2
8. 39 cm^2 **9.** 20 cm^2 **10.** 75 cm^2 **11.** 36 mm^2 **12.** 48 cm^2

Exercise 3   *page 51*

1. 36 cm^2 **2.** 29 cm^2 **3.** 51 cm^2 **4.** 36 cm^2 **5.** 24 cm^2 **6.** 24 cm^2 **7.** 57 cm^2
8. 48 cm^2 **9.** 36 cm^2 **10.** 41 cm^2

Exercise 4   *page 52*

1.   (a) 14.6 m   (b) 6   (c) £19.20   (d) 11.22 m^2
2. A. (a) 13.2 m   (b) 6   (c) £19.20   (d) 9.32 m^2
       B. (a) 15.6 m   (b) 8   (c) £25.60   (d) 11.17 m^2
       C. (a) 9.4 m   (b) 4   (c) £12.80   (d) 3.76 m^2
       D. (a) 19.4 m   (b) 9   (c) £28.80   (d) 13 m^2

Exercise 5   *page 53*

1. All in square units   (b) 10, 6, 3   (c) 36   (d) 17   2. (b) 5, 14, 6   (c) 42   (d) 17
3. $13\frac{1}{2}$ 4. $14\frac{1}{2}$ 5. $21\frac{1}{2}$ 6. 15   7. $17\frac{1}{2}$ 8. 24   9. 22
10. 21   11. 12   12. 14   13. 28   14. 29

Exercise 6   *page 54*

1. 34.6 cm   2. 25.1 cm   3. 37.7 cm   4. 15.7 cm   5. 28.3 cm   6. 53.4 m
7. 44.6 m   8. 72.3 m   9. 52.2 m   10. 78.5 m   11. 56.5 km   12. 47.1 cm
13. 3.27 m   14. 2.98 m   15. 19.5 m   16. 25.8 km   17. 5.28 mm   18. 11.7 cm
19. 57.2 m   20. 19.5 mm   21. 15.1 miles   22. 26.1 feet   23. 24.5 km   24. 0.289 m
25. 8.98 cm

Exercise 7   *page 55*

1. 23.1 cm   2. 38.6 cm   3. 20.6 m   4. 8.23 cm   5. 129 m   6. 56.6 cm
7. 28.6 cm   8. 39.4 m   9. 53.7 m   10. 28.1 m   11. 24.8 cm   12. 46.3 m
13. 28.8 cm   14. 51.7 m

Exercise 8   *page 57*

1. 95.0 cm^2 2. 78.5 cm^2 3. 28.3 m^2 4. 38.5 m^2 5. 113 cm^2 6. 201 cm^2
7. 19.6 m^2 8. 380 cm^2 9. 346 m^2 10. 314 cm^2 11. 18.1 km^2 12. 5.31 m^2
13. 296 cm^2 14. 284 km^2 15. 52.8 cm^2 16. 0.126 m^2 17. 106 m^2 18. 10.2 cm^2
19. 2.27 m^2 20. 11.9 km^2

Exercise 9   *page 58*

1. 25.1 cm^2 2. 14.1 cm^2 3. 56.5 m^2 4. 0.393 m^2 5. 127 m^2 6. 6.28 cm^2
7. 19.6 cm^2 8. 95.0 m^2 9. 0.385 m^2 10. 157 m^2 11. 88.4 cm^2

Exercise 10   *page 59*

1. 18.3 cm^2 2. 19.9 cm^2 3. 43.4 cm^2 4. 37.7 cm^2 5. 28.3 cm^2
6. 74.6 cm^2 7. 3.43 cm^2 8. 17.4 cm^2
9. (a) 12.5 cm^2 (b) 50 cm^2 (c) 78.5 cm^2 (d) 28.5 cm^2
10. (a) 4.5   (b) 18   (c) 28.3   (d) 10.3

Exercise 11   *page 60*

1. 36 cm^3 2. 40 cm^3 3. 50 cm^3 4. 84 m^3 5. 5000 cm^3
6. 0.1 cm^3 7. 93 cm^3 8. 0.84 m^3 9. $\frac{1}{2}$ cm   10. $3\frac{1}{2}$ cm
11. $5\frac{1}{4}$ cm   12. 0.2 cm   13. 10 cm^3 14. 12 cm^3 15. 18 cm^3
16. 22 cm^3 17. 21 cm^3 18. 12 cm^3 19. 18 cm^3

Exercise 12   *page 62*

1. 150 cm^3 2. 60 m^3 3. 480 cm^3 4. 60 m^3 5. 300 cm^3
6. 56 m^3 7. 340 cm^3 8. 145 cm^3 9. 448 cm^3 10. 108 cm^3

Exercise 13   *page 63*

1. 62.8 cm^3 2. 113 cm^3 3. 198 cm^3 4. 763 cm^3 5. 157 cm^3
6. 385 cm^3 7. 770 cm^3 8. 176 m^3 9. 228 m^3 10. 486 cm^3
11. 0.665 m^3 12. 17.6 cm^3 13. 5.99 m^3 14. 29.8 m^3 15. 118 ft^3
16. 99.5 ft^3 17. 876 in^3 18. 32.6 cm^3

Exercise 14   *page 64*

1. (a) 2400 cm³   (b) 0.0024 m³   **2.** (a) 200 m²   (b) 2400 m³
3. 770 cm³   **4.** (a) 2.25 cm²   (b) 0.451 cm³   (c) 4510 cm³
5. 25   **6.** (a) 76 cm²   (b) 30 400 cm³   (c) 237 kg   (d) 33
7. 8 cm³   **8.** (a) 7   (b) 35, 6   (c) 1200 cm³, 14 000 cm³   (d) 48p, £5.60, £50.40   (e) 140

PART 5

Exercise 1   *page 66*

1. −4°C   **2.** −6°C   **3.** 5°C
4. (a) 4°C   (b) −3°C   (c) 5°C   (d) −8°C   (e) 2°C   (f) −3°C   (g) −4°C
     (h) 1°C   (i) 2°C   (j) −5°C   (k) 12°C   (l) −3°C   (m) +4°C   (n) +5°C
     (o) −6°C   (p) +6°C   (q) +3°C   (r) +8°C   (s) 10°C   (t) 3°C   (u) 3°C
     (v) 11°C   (w) 3°C   (x) −5°C   (y) −6°C   (z) −10°C

Exercise 2   *page 67*

1. T	**2.** T	**3.** T	**4.** F	**5.** F	**6.** T	**7.** F
8. T	**9.** F	**10.** T	**11.** F	**12.** F	**13.** T	**14.** T
15. T	**16.** T	**17.** F	**18.** F	**19.** T	**20.** F	**21.** <
22. >	**23.** >	**24.** >	**25.** <	**26.** <	**27.** >	**28.** >
29. <	**30.** >	**31.** >	**32.** >	**33.** <	**34.** >	**35.** <
36. <	**37.** >	**38.** >	**39.** >	**40.** >		

41. −4, −3, −2	**42.** −5, −3, 7	**43.** −5, 0, 5	**44.** −8, −3, 1
45. −4, −2, −1	**46.** −4, −3, 2, 6	**47.** −2, −1, 1, 3	**48.** −3, −2, 0, 4
49. −5, −3, 1, 4	**50.** −7, −3, 2, 7	**51.** −4, −1, 0, 4	**52.** −6, −2, −1, 2
53. −4, −1, 5, 6	**54.** −8, −4, −1, 10	**55.** −8, −3, 0, 1, 7	**56.** −9, −6, −5, 0, 1
57. −3, −2, −1, 4, 5	**58.** −9, −2, −1, 6, 8	**59.** −4, −3, 1, 4, 5	**60.** −60, −20, −6, 2, 17
61. 2, 0	**62.** 3, 0	**63.** −2, −3	**64.** −4, −6
65. −6, −12	**66.** 0, 1	**67.** −2, 0	**68.** −2, −6
69. −15, −25	**70.** 2, 6	**71.** 2, 5	**72.** −6, −10
73. 12, 17	**74.** 2, −3	**75.** 10, 15	**76.** −6, −11
77. 0, 5	**78.** −7, −10	**79.** −18, −32	**80.** 1, 5

Exercise 3   *page 67*

1. 4	**2.** −3	**3.** 6	**4.** −4	**5.** 7	**6.** 5	**7.** −6
8. −6	**9.** −2	**10.** 1	**11.** 0	**12.** −13	**13.** −16	**14.** 1
15. 0	**16.** 3	**17.** −10	**18.** −5	**19.** −1	**20.** −2	**21.** −10
22. −4	**23.** −13	**24.** −20	**25.** −10	**26.** −9	**27.** −7	**28.** −5
29. 2	**30.** 1	**31.** −11	**32.** −14	**33.** −13	**34.** −5	**35.** −2
36. −12	**37.** −23	**38.** −23	**39.** −22	**40.** 3	**41.** −18	**42.** −11
43. −93	**44.** −90	**45.** 24	**46.** −46	**47.** −20	**48.** −18	**49.** −10
50. 0	**51.** −11	**52.** −11	**53.** −53	**54.** −99	**55.** 30	**56.** −20
57. −41	**58.** −1	**59.** −21	**60.** 2			

Exercise 4   *page 68*

1. 1	**2.** 4	**3.** 4	**4.** 14	**5.** 10	**6.** 2	**7.** 1
8. −14	**9.** −8	**10.** −5	**11.** −4	**12.** −1	**13.** 7	**14.** 5
15. 2	**16.** −5	**17.** −20	**18.** −15	**19.** −2	**20.** 16	**21.** −11
22. 6	**23.** −8	**24.** −6	**25.** −2	**26.** −17	**27.** 0	**28.** −16
29. 6	**30.** 15	**31.** 16	**32.** −3	**33.** −8	**34.** −7	**35.** −10
36. 17	**37.** −12	**38.** 0	**39.** 2	**40.** 95		

Exercise 5   *page 68*

1. −6	**2.** −4	**3.** −15	**4.** 9	**5.** −8	**6.** −15	**7.** −24
8. 6	**9.** 12	**10.** −18	**11.** −21	**12.** 25	**13.** −60	**14.** 21
15. 48	**16.** −16	**17.** −42	**18.** 20	**19.** −42	**20.** −66	**21.** −4
22. −3	**23.** 3	**24.** −5	**25.** 4	**26.** −4	**27.** −4	**28.** −1
29. −2	**30.** 4	**31.** −16	**32.** −2	**33.** −4	**34.** 5	**35.** −10
36. 11	**37.** 16	**38.** −2	**39.** −4	**40.** −5	**41.** 64	**42.** −27
43. −600	**44.** 40	**45.** 2	**46.** 36	**47.** −2	**48.** −8	**49.** 160
50. −2						

Exercise 6   *page 68*

1. −4	**2.** −12	**3.** 1	**4.** −4	**5.** 16	**6.** −13	**7.** 2
8. −3	**9.** −6	**10.** 0	**11.** −12	**12.** 8	**13.** −4	**14.** −100
15. −12	**16.** −5	**17.** −2	**18.** −11	**19.** −20	**20.** 5	**21.** −6
22. −9	**23.** −1	**24.** 9	**25.** 6	**26.** 0	**27.** −5	**28.** −15
29. 12	**30.** −4					

Exercise 7   *page 68*

1. −27	**2.** −13	**3.** −10	**4.** 1	**5.** −2	**6.** 0	**7.** 0
8. −400	**9.** 16	**10.** 42	**11.** −1	**12.** 33	**13.** 15	**14.** −60
15. −13	**16.** −11	**17.** 200	**18.** 52	**19.** −44	**20.** 0	**21.** −9
22. −49	**23.** −10	**24.** −38	**25.** −20	**26.** 501		

Exercise 8   *page 69*

1.

add	−2	1	4	0	−3	6	−1	5
−3	−5	−2	1	−3	−6	3	−4	2
2	0	3	6	2	−1	8	1	7
4	2	5	8	4	1	10	3	9
−2	−4	−1	2	−2	−5	4	−3	3
−1	−3	0	3	−1	−4	5	−2	4
5	3	6	9	5	2	11	4	10
−4	−6	−3	0	−4	−7	2	−5	1
1	−1	2	5	1	−2	7	0	6

2.

multiply	−2	5	2	6	−4	0	−3	3
3	−6	15	6	18	−12	0	−9	9
−1	2	−5	−2	−6	4	0	3	−3
−2	4	−10	−4	−12	8	0	6	−6
4	−8	20	8	24	−16	0	−12	12
5	−10	25	10	30	−20	0	−15	15
−4	8	−20	−8	−24	16	0	12	−12
1	−2	5	2	6	−4	0	−3	3
−3	6	−15	−6	−18	12	0	9	−9

Exercise 9   *page 69*

1. $3x + 6$	**2.** $5x + 7$	**3.** $2x - 4$	**4.** $3x + 10$	**5.** $6y + 3$
6. $2y - 7$	**7.** $5m - 8$	**8.** $6x - y$	**9.** $3y + t$	**10.** $6p - a$
11. $3(x + 4)$	**12.** $5(x + 3)$	**13.** $6(y + 11)$	**14.** $9(m - 5)$	**15.** $5t - 7$
16. $4(x - 6)$	**17.** $\dfrac{x + 3}{4}$	**18.** $\dfrac{x - 7}{3}$	**19.** $\dfrac{y - 8}{5}$	**20.** $\dfrac{x + m}{7}$
21. $3(2x + 7)$	**22.** $\dfrac{3x - y}{5}$	**23.** $\dfrac{2(4a + 3)}{5}$	**24.** $\dfrac{3(m - 6)}{4}$	**25.** $\dfrac{4(t + x)}{5}$
26. $x^2 + 4$	**27.** $x^2 - 6$	**28.** $\dfrac{x^2 + 3}{4}$	**29.** $(n + 2)^2$	**30.** $(w - x)^2$

31. $(y + t)^2$ **32.** $\dfrac{x^2 - 7}{3}$ **33.** $3x^2 + 4$ **34.** $2(y^2 + 4)$ **35.** $\dfrac{a^3 - 3}{7}$

36. $\dfrac{z^3 + 6}{8}$ **37.** $4(p^2 - x)$ **38.** $(x - 9)^2 + 10$ **39.** $\dfrac{(y + 7)^2}{x}$ **40.** $\dfrac{(a - x)^3}{y}$

Exercise 10   page 70

1. $(x + y - 7)$ cm   **2.** $(l + t - 10)$ cm   **3.** $(l - 3)$ cm
4. $(15 - x)$ cm   **5.** £$(c + 195)$ **6.** $(x + 25 - y)$ pence
7. $3n + 55$ **8.** $(c + w + 2000)$ m   **9.** $(y + d + x)$ cm
10. $(2t + 3)$ km, $(3t + 3)$ km   **11.** £ $2x + 100$ **12.** $(l + 200 - m)$ kg
13. $4(n + 2)$ **14.** $6w$ kg   **15.** xl kg
16. $\dfrac{n}{6}$ pence   **17.** £$\dfrac{p}{5}$ **18.** $\dfrac{12}{n}$ kg
19. $\dfrac{m}{4}$ kg   **20.** $3x - 11$

Exercise 11   page 71

1.

1	2	0	5	−5
4	1	5	7	11
3	0	1	−2	−1
−4	4	2	9	10
−4	5	−3	6	3

2.

5	1	0	1	−1
−5	0	0	0	8
−4	1	2	1	2
7	−5	6	5	7
4	−1	6	6	−6

3.

−6	−8	−4	−6	6
0	−2	6	10	30
−10	−9	−12	0	0
3	−12	−15	18	24
4	0	2	8	0

Exercise 12   page 72

1. 4   **2.** −4   **3.** 4   **4.** 12   **5.** 8   **6.** −5   **7.** 7
8. 3   **9.** 6   **10.** 12   **11.** −2   **12.** 14   **13.** 4   **14.** 15
15. −2   **16.** −3   **17.** 7   **18.** −4   **19.** 2   **20.** 10   **21.** 5
22. 2   **23.** −4   **24.** 10   **25.** 9   **26.** −2   **27.** −8   **28.** 2
29. 0   **30.** 15   **31.** 2   **32.** −8   **33.** 4   **34.** 11   **35.** −14
36. −15   **37.** 4   **38.** 0   **39.** 5   **40.** −4

Exercise 13   page 72

1. 2   **2.** −3   **3.** −3   **4.** 2   **5.** 5   **6.** −6   **7.** −1
8. 1   **9.** 5   **10.** 10   **11.** 5   **12.** 13   **13.** 3   **14.** 13
15. −3   **16.** −5   **17.** 6   **18.** 3   **19.** 10   **20.** 7   **21.** 1
22. −5   **23.** 4   **24.** 4   **25.** −3   **26.** −1   **27.** −7   **28.** 5
29. 6   **30.** 9   **31.** −3   **32.** −1   **33.** −3   **34.** 0   **35.** −6
36. −14   **37.** 11   **38.** −12   **39.** 4   **40.** 1

Exercise 14   page 72

1. −9   **2.** −8   **3.** 8   **4.** 8   **5.** 24   **6.** 6   **7.** −9
8. −27   **9.** −4   **10.** −18   **11.** −16   **12.** −4   **13.** −6   **14.** 6
15. −15   **16.** 20   **17.** −6   **18.** 28   **19.** 8   **20.** 6   **21.** −12
22. 36   **23.** −20   **24.** −8   **25.** 12   **26.** −6   **27.** −6   **28.** 12
29. −10   **30.** 6   **31.** −3   **32.** −22   **33.** −12   **34.** 20   **35.** −18
36. −21   **37.** −4   **38.** 40   **39.** 15   **40.** 27   **41.** 16   **42.** −4
43. 16   **44.** −6   **45.** −11   **46.** −8   **47.** 4   **48.** 2   **49.** 9
50. 33   **51.** 3   **52.** −30   **53.** 30   **54.** 21   **55.** −10   **56.** 44
57. −3   **58.** −2   **59.** 12   **60.** −2

Exercise 15   page 72

1. 15	**2.** −8	**3.** 4	**4.** −12	**5.** 12	**6.** −9	**7.** −35
8. 45	**9.** −12	**10.** 30	**11.** −32	**12.** −24	**13.** −36	**14.** −20
15. 25	**16.** −30	**17.** −15	**18.** 14	**19.** −6	**20.** −14	**21.** 20
22. 18	**23.** −40	**24.** −16	**25.** 6	**26.** 10	**27:** 28	**28.** −14
29. −20	**30.** 21	**31.** −18	**32.** −44	**33.** 10	**34.** 10	**35.** −36
36. 35	**37.** −8	**38.** 20	**39.** −35	**40.** −63	**41.** −24	**42.** 12
43. 8	**44.** −12	**45.** −66	**46.** −48	**47.** −6	**48.** 24	**49.** −21
50. −77	**51.** −30	**52.** 50	**53.** −70	**54.** −49	**55.** −60	**56.** 22
57. 42	**58.** −12	**59.** −28	**60.** 18			

Exercise 16   page 72

1. −5	**2.** 8	**3.** −17	**4.** 8	**5.** −2	**6.** −27	**7.** 1
8. −22	**9.** −22	**10.** −22	**11.** −10	**12.** −2	**13.** 23	**14.** −44
15. 26	**16.** 25	**17.** −4	**18.** 0	**19.** −16	**20.** 22	**21.** −5
22. 30	**23.** 13	**24.** 25	**25.** 40	**26.** 3	**27.** −5	**28.** −12
29. −34	**30.** 2	**31.** 12	**32.** 39	**33.** 40	**34.** 7	**35.** 3
36. 10	**37.** 51	**38.** −2	**39.** 1	**40.** 11	**41.** 10	**42.** 1
43. −20	**44.** −21	**45.** 16	**46.** −14	**47.** −5	**48.** −25	**49.** −45
50. −23						

Exercise 17   page 73

1. 9	**2.** −13	**3.** 11	**4.** 0	**5.** 14	**6.** 15	**7.** 6
8. 13	**9.** 28	**10.** 24	**11.** 8	**12.** −6	**13.** −5	**14.** 48
15. −16	**16.** −3	**17.** 17	**18.** 5	**19.** 7	**20.** 1	**21.** 1
22. −15	**23.** −11	**24.** −6	**25.** −9	**26.** 0	**27.** 25	**28.** 13
29. 13	**30.** −12	**31.** −22	**32.** −24	**33.** −2	**34.** −2	**35.** 0
36. −25	**37.** −6	**38.** 10	**39.** 16	**40.** −13	**41.** 13	**42.** −26
43. −20	**44.** 16	**45.** 18	**46.** −21	**47.** −31	**48.** 42	**49.** −38
50. 19						

Exercise 18   page 73

1. 4	**2.** 4	**3.** 9	**4.** 16	**5.** 8	**6.** −8	**7.** −27
8. 64	**9.** 8	**10.** 16	**11.** 8	**12.** 16	**13.** 18	**14.** 36
15. 48	**16.** 16	**17.** 20	**18.** 54	**19.** 144	**20.** 24	**21.** 13
22. 10	**23.** 1	**24.** 18	**25.** 13	**26.** 19	**27.** 10	**28.** 32
29. 16	**30.** 144	**31.** 36	**32.** 36	**33.** 4	**34.** 1	**35.** 2
36. −14	**37.** −5	**38.** −5	**39.** −10	**40.** 10	**41.** 0	**42.** 4
43. 50	**44.** 4	**45.** −10	**46.** −4	**47.** −6	**48.** −16	**49.** 28
50. 44	**51.** 2	**52.** −1	**53.** −1	**54.** 3	**55.** $\frac{1}{2}$	**56.** 1

Exercise 19   page 73

1. 1	**2.** 16	**3.** 9	**4.** 25	**5.** −1	**6.** −64	**7.** 27
8. −125	**9.** 2	**10.** 4	**11.** 32	**12.** 64	**13.** 18	**14.** 36
15. 75	**16.** 4	**17.** 80	**18.** 54	**19.** 225	**20.** −3	**21.** 13
22. 19	**23.** 13	**24.** 9	**25.** 25	**26.** 19	**27.** −11	**28.** −25
29. 16	**30.** 225	**31.** 144	**32.** −45	**33.** 3	**34.** −7	**35.** −4
36. −26	**37.** −1	**38.** 7	**39.** −7	**40.** −17	**41.** −15	**42.** −8
43. −55	**44.** −8	**45.** 1	**46.** −10	**47.** −12	**48.** 28	**49.** −8
50. 128	**51.** −4$\frac{2}{3}$	**52.** −4$\frac{1}{2}$	**53.** −$\frac{1}{5}$	**54.** 1	**55.** −$\frac{1}{4}$	**56.** $\frac{8}{11}$

Exercise 20   *page 74*

1. $5x + 8$ **2.** $9x + 5$ **3.** $7x + 4$ **4.** $7x + 4$
5. $7x + 7$ **6.** $8x + 12$ **7.** $12x - 6$ **8.** $2x + 5$
9. $2x - 5$ **10.** $2x - 5$ **11.** $9x - 9$ **12.** $3x - 5$
13. $9x + 6$ **14.** $13x$ **15.** 6 **16.** $7y - 2$
17. $10y - 2$ **18.** $4y$ **19.** -8 **20.** $4y + 8$
21. $13a + 3b - 1$ **22.** $10m + 3n + 8$ **23.** $3p - 2q - 8$ **24.** $2s - 7t + 14$
25. $2a + 1$ **26.** $x + y + 7z$ **27.** $5x - 4y + 4z$ **28.** $5k - 4m$
29. $4a + 5b - 9$ **30.** $a - 4x - 5e$

Exercise 21   *page 74*

1. $x^2 + 7x + 3$ **2.** $x^2 + 7x + 8$ **3.** $x^2 + 3x + 3$ **4.** $3x^2 + 6x + 5$
5. $2x^2 + 6x - 7$ **6.** $3x^2 + x + 12$ **7.** $2x^2 + x + 3$ **8.** $2x^2 - x$
9. $x^2 - 4x - 2$ **10.** $3x^2 - 2x - 2$ **11.** $8a + 9$ **12.** $2m^2 + 8m - 10$
13. $10 + x - 3x^2$ **14.** $2 - 4x - 3x^2$ **15.** $22 + 4t + 2t^2$ **16.** 23
17. 4 **18.** $4x^2 - 7x + 29$ **19.** $4 - x - 2x^2$ **20.** $11x$
21. $x^2 + 5xy + 5x$ **22.** $4x^2 + 6xy - 2x$ **23.** $7x^2 + 8xy + x$ **24.** $5x^2 + 2xy + x$
25. $4x^2 + 3xy + x$ **26.** $4m^2 + 3mn + 2m$ **27.** $8a^2 - 5a + 4ab$ **28.** $6cd$
29. $3z^2 + 10xz + 5z$ **30.** $4p^2 - 10p$ **31.** $5x^2 + 4y^2 + x$ **32.** $x + 12$
33. $5y^2 - 6y + 2$ **34.** $3ab - 3b$ **35.** $2cd - 2d^2$ **36.** $4ab - 2a^2 + 2a$
37. $2x^3 + 5x^2$ **38.** $x^3 + x^2 + 11$ **39.** $3xy$ **40.** $p^2 - q^2$

Exercise 22   *page 75*

1. $2x + 8$ **2.** $5 + x + y$ **3.** $16 + x + y$ **4.** $3l + 13$
5. $3x + d + 11$ **6.** $4t + m + 3$ **7.** $3a + b + 3$ **8.** $6x + 2y + 12$
9. $10x + 8$

Exercise 23   *page 75*

1. $6x$ **2.** $8x$ **3.** $6x$ **4.** $15x$ **5.** $6y$ **6.** $20y$
7. $21x$ **8.** $-6x$ **9.** $-20x$ **10.** $-10x$ **11.** $28a$ **12.** $15a$
13. $6x$ **14.** $12y$ **15.** $25y$ **16.** $2x^2$ **17.** $4x^2$ **18.** $6x^2$
19. $3y^2$ **20.** $10y^2$ **21.** $7x^2$ **22.** $5a^2$ **23.** $6x^2$ **24.** $12x^2$
25. $10x^2$ **26.** $8x^2$ **27.** $14x^2$ **28.** $18x^2$ **29.** $10y^2$ **30.** $24t^2$
31. $2x^3$ **32.** $6x^3$ **33.** $4y^3$ **34.** $6a^3$ **35.** $9y^3$ **36.** $5x^3$
37. $21p^2$ **38.** $12x^2$ **39.** $60x^2$ **40.** $30x^2$ **41.** $30x^3$ **42.** $12x^3$
43. $4x^3$ **44.** $12y^2$ **45.** $12a^3$ **46.** $3x^4$ **47.** $2xy$ **48.** $6a^3$
49. $6ab$ **50.** $10pq$ **51.** $15xy$ **52.** $18x^3$ **53.** $24a^4$ **54.** $36x^3$
55. $2a^2b$ **56.** $3xy^2$ **57.** $5c^2d$ **58.** a^2b^2 **59.** $2x^2y^2$ **60.** $6cd$

Exercise 24   *page 76*

1. $6x^2 \text{ cm}^2$ **2.** $10x^2 \text{ cm}^2$ **3.** $4x^2 \text{ cm}^2$ **4.** $9y^2 \text{ cm}^2$ **5.** $9x^2 \text{ cm}^2$ **6.** $12d^2 \text{ cm}^2$
7. $10x^2 \text{ cm}^2$ **8.** $26x^2 \text{ cm}^2$ **9.** $18z^2 \text{ cm}^2$

Exercise 25   *page 76*

1. $6x^2 \text{ cm}^2$ $2x + 6$ **2.** $3x + 15$ **3.** $4x + 24$ **4.** $4x + 2$ **5.** $10x + 15$
6. $12x - 4$ **7.** $12x - 12$ **8.** $15x - 6$ **9.** $15x - 20$ **10.** $14x - 21$
11. $4x + 6$ **12.** $6x + 3$ **13.** $5x + 20$ **14.** $12x + 12$ **15.** $4x + 12$
16. $12x + 84$ **17.** $6x - 9$ **18.** $10x + 40$ **19.** $18x + 45$ **20.** $24x - 48$
21. $-4x - 6$ **22.** $-8x - 4$ **23.** $-3x - 6$ **24.** $-6x - 8$ **25.** $-8x + 2$
26. $-10x + 10$ **27.** $-6x - 3$ **28.** $-2x - 1$ **29.** $-3x - 2$ **30.** $-4x + 5$
31. $x^2 + 3x$ **32.** $x^2 + 5x$ **33.** $x^2 - 2x$ **34.** $x^2 - 3x$ **35.** $2x^2 + x$
36. $3x^2 - 2x$ **37.** $3x^2 + 5x$ **38.** $2x^2 - 2x$ **39.** $2x^2 + 4x$ **40.** $6x^2 + 9x$

Exercise 26   *page 77*

1. (a) $2x - 2$ (b) $3x - 1$ (c) $x - 1$ (d) $x + 2$ (e) $x - 3$ (f) $x + 3$
   (g) $x + 3$
2. (a) $3x + 3$ (b) $4x + 6$ (c) $x + 5$ (d) $2x + 1$ (e) $2x - 2$ (f) 7
   (g) $x + 6$ (h) $x + 7$ (i) $x + 5$

PART 6

Exercise 1   *page 79*

1. 8	**2.** 10	**3.** 13	**4.** 3	**5.** 5	**6.** 6	**7.** 4
8. 1	**9.** 8	**10.** −2	**11.** −3	**12.** −5	**13.** 2	**14.** −2
15. 10	**16.** −5	**17.** 1	**18.** −10	**19.** 5	**20.** 2	**21.** 16
22. −8	**23.** 4	**24.** −6	**25.** 5	**26.** 12	**27.** 11	**28.** 19
29. −6	**30.** 23	**31.** 9	**32.** 12	**33.** −16	**34.** 1	**35.** 5
36. −12						

Exercise 2   *page 79*

1. 3	**2.** 6	**3.** 7	**4.** 6	**5.** 8	**6.** 9
7. 9	**8.** 10	**9.** 30	**10.** 5	**11.** 100	**12.** 12
13. $\frac{2}{5}$	**14.** $\frac{5}{7}$	**15.** $\frac{3}{8}$	**16.** $\frac{1}{4}$	**17.** $\frac{1}{2}$	**18.** $\frac{5}{9}$
19. $1\frac{2}{3}$	**20.** $1\frac{3}{4}$	**21.** $2\frac{1}{3}$	**22.** $4\frac{1}{2}$	**23.** $3\frac{1}{3}$	**24.** $2\frac{1}{5}$
25. $-\frac{4}{5}$	**26.** −4	**27.** −2	**28.** −9	**29.** $-\frac{2}{3}$	**30.** $-\frac{1}{12}$
31. $-1\frac{3}{7}$	**32.** $\frac{1}{5}$	**33.** $-2\frac{1}{4}$	**34.** −1	**35.** −1	**36.** −4
37. 2	**38.** 5	**39.** 4	**40.** 8	**41.** $1\frac{1}{5}$	**42.** $7\frac{1}{2}$
43. −4	**44.** $-3\frac{1}{2}$	**45.** −3	**46.** −3	**47.** 10	**48.** 10

Exercise 3   *page 80*

1. 12	**2.** 20	**3.** 20	**4.** 28	**5.** 72	**6.** −12
7. −4	**8.** 0	**9.** 1	**10.** 360	**11.** 1	**12.** 2
13. $3\frac{1}{2}$	**14.** 2	**15.** 70	**16.** 35	**17.** 36	**18.** 77
19. −9	**20.** −8	**21.** −5	**22.** −80	**23.** −160	**24.** $\frac{1}{2}$
25. 20	**26.** 7	**27.** 16	**28.** 45		

Exercise 4   *page 80*

1. 3	**2.** 2	**3.** 2	**4.** 6	**5.** 2	**6.** 4
7. $2\frac{1}{2}$	**8.** 4	**9.** $\frac{3}{4}$	**10.** $1\frac{1}{5}$	**11.** $2\frac{3}{5}$	**12.** $1\frac{1}{3}$
13. $\frac{1}{2}$	**14.** 1	**15.** $-\frac{1}{2}$	**16.** −1	**17.** 0	**18.** $\frac{2}{3}$
19. $\frac{4}{5}$	**20.** $-\frac{4}{7}$	**21.** $\frac{7}{9}$	**22.** $\frac{3}{10}$	**23.** $2\frac{4}{5}$	**24.** $-\frac{5}{6}$
25. $-2\frac{1}{3}$	**26.** $1\frac{1}{2}$	**27.** $-2\frac{1}{2}$	**28.** 2	**29.** 4	**30.** $3\frac{1}{4}$
31. $\frac{5}{8}$	**32.** $-1\frac{1}{5}$	**33.** $-\frac{1}{7}$	**34.** $-1\frac{3}{5}$	**35.** −3	**36.** −2
37. $3\frac{1}{2}$	**38.** 2	**39.** 3	**40.** 1	**41.** $\frac{1}{3}$	**42.** −2
43. $3\frac{1}{3}$	**44.** $-1\frac{1}{2}$	**45.** $\frac{1}{10}$	**46.** $-\frac{2}{11}$	**47.** 4	**48.** 0

Exercise 5   *page 81*

1. 2	**2.** 3	**3.** 1	**4.** 2	**5.** 4	**6.** 3
7. $\frac{1}{2}$	**8.** 1	**9.** 2	**10.** 5	**11.** 3	**12.** 2
13. 4	**14.** 1	**15.** 1	**16.** $\frac{1}{2}$	**17.** $\frac{9}{10}$	**18.** 8
19. 7	**20.** $2\frac{2}{3}$	**21.** 8	**22.** $\frac{5}{12}$	**23.** $\frac{3}{4}$	**24.** $\frac{8}{9}$
25. 5	**26.** 6	**27.** $-\frac{1}{2}$	**28.** −7	**29.** −8	**30.** −2

Exercise 6   *page 81*

1. $2\frac{1}{2}$	**2.** $\frac{1}{3}$	**3.** $2\frac{1}{4}$	**4.** 5	**5.** $1\frac{1}{2}$	**6.** 1
7. 1	**8.** $2\frac{2}{3}$	**9.** $2\frac{1}{10}$	**10.** $\frac{1}{2}$	**11.** 1	**12.** 2
13. 2	**14.** 2	**15.** 1	**16.** 4	**17.** 2	**18.** -1
19. -3	**20.** -4	**21.** 5	**22.** 9	**23.** $-2\frac{1}{3}$	**24.** $\frac{2}{5}$
25. $\frac{3}{5}$	**26.** -1	**27.** 13	**28.** 9	**29.** $4\frac{1}{2}$	**30.** $3\frac{1}{3}$

Exercise 7   *page 81*

1. $\frac{3}{5}$	**2.** $\frac{3}{4}$	**3.** $4\frac{1}{2}$	**4.** 2	**5.** $5\frac{1}{2}$	**6.** $2\frac{1}{3}$
7. $\frac{3}{8}$	**8.** 7	**9.** $-\frac{3}{7}$	**10.** $-\frac{3}{10}$	**11.** $-\frac{1}{2}$	**12.** 1
13. 5	**14.** $1\frac{2}{3}$	**15.** 3	**16.** $\frac{1}{2}$	**17.** $4\frac{3}{5}$	**18.** $4\frac{1}{2}$
19. $2\frac{3}{7}$	**20.** $-2\frac{2}{3}$				

Exercise 8   *page 82*

1. 3	**2.** $1\frac{1}{2}$	**3.** 4	**4.** 5	**5.** 2	**6.** $\frac{2}{3}$
7. 1	**8.** $\frac{2}{3}$	**9.** 1	**10.** $\frac{1}{2}$	**11.** 2	**12.** $\frac{4}{5}$
13. 3	**14.** 2	**15.** -9	**16.** 13	**17.** $3\frac{2}{3}$	**18.** $-\frac{1}{2}$
19. 3	**20.** $10\frac{2}{3}$				

Exercise 9   *page 83*

1. $\frac{3}{4}$ **2.** $\frac{1}{4}$ **3.** $1\frac{4}{5}$ **4.** $\frac{3}{7}$ **5.** $1\frac{3}{8}$ **6.** $1\frac{1}{4}$ **7.** 7

8. (a) $3\frac{3}{5}$ (b) $\frac{3}{4}$ **9.** (a) $\frac{2}{3}$ (b) $4\frac{1}{2}$ **10.** width = 7 cm, area = 84cm^2

11. (a) 41   (b) 31   **12.** 29   **13.** (a) 53   (b) 65   **14.** 55p

15. (c) 32, 56, 208   (d) 16   (e) $n = 4x$

Exercise 10   *page 84*

1. C	**2.** B	**3.** C	**4.** D	**5.** C	**6.** B	**7.** C
8. D	**9.** A	**10.** A	**11.** C	**12.** D	**13.** B	**14.** C
15. A	**16.** C	**17.** B	**18.** B	**19.** C	**20.** D	

Exercise 11   *page 85*

1. $c - a$	**2.** $m - d$	**3.** $m - h$	**4.** $t - e$
5. $q + m$	**6.** $m + k$	**7.** $a + b + n$	**8.** $c + b - B$
9. $a + d - D$	**10.** $m + t + M$	**11.** $u - w + v$	**12.** $t - s - T$
13. $n - B$	**14.** $m - M$	**15.** $a - b - N$	**16.** $v - n - R$
17. $y^2 - K$	**18.** $b^2 + a^2$	**19.** $N^2 + n^2$	**20.** $-a - p$
21. $a + n$	**22.** $mn - r$	**23.** $c - m$	**24.** $B + b$
25. $a - b + c$	**26.** $e - c + d$	**27.** $c^2 - a^2 + b^2$	**28.** $m^2 - mn + v^2$
29. $b + a + t$	**30.** $f + g + h$	**31.** $b + B^2 + B$	**32.** $2a - A$
33. $T^2 + 2t$	**34.** $w - w^3$	**35.** $uv - w^2$	**36.** $T^3 - t^3$
37. $a^3 + abc$	**38.** $mn^2 - m^3$	**39.** $a + 2bc$	**40.** $3pq$

Exercise 12   *page 85*

1. 4	**2.** 6	**3.** $\frac{c}{a}$	**4.** $\frac{t}{m}$	**5.** $\frac{m}{M}$
6. $\frac{a}{t}$	**7.** $\frac{n}{m}$	**8.** $\frac{L}{x}$	**9.** $\frac{n^2}{m^2}$	**10.** $\frac{h}{q}$
11. $\frac{A}{ab}$	**12.** $\frac{M^2}{m^2}$	**13.** $\frac{c}{a}$	**14.** $\frac{x}{t}$	**15.** $\frac{v}{d}$

16. $\dfrac{u^2}{v^2}$ **17.** $\dfrac{b}{t^2}$ **18.** $\dfrac{B}{b}$ **19.** $\dfrac{c}{e}$ **20.** $\dfrac{a}{k^2}$

21. $\dfrac{a+b}{x}$ **22.** $\dfrac{e-f}{m}$ **23.** $\dfrac{s+t}{n}$ **24.** $\dfrac{p+q}{H}$ **25.** $\dfrac{ab+c}{z}$

26. $\dfrac{a^2-b^2}{v}$ **27.** $\dfrac{pq}{M}$ **28.** $\dfrac{km-m^2}{n}$ **29.** $\dfrac{c-k}{x^2}$ **30.** $\dfrac{a-b-A}{p}$

31. $\dfrac{A}{xz}$ **32.** $\dfrac{B}{wv}$ **33.** $\dfrac{Ba}{dk}$ **34.** $\dfrac{1}{n^2m^2}$ **35.** $\dfrac{m}{x^2}$

36. $\dfrac{A}{p^2}$ **37.** $\dfrac{N}{n^2}$ **38.** $\dfrac{A}{BL}$ **39.** $\dfrac{a+b}{cP}$ **40.** $\dfrac{e+t}{kQ}$

41. $a-t$ **42.** $v+m^2$ **43.** $b-k$ **44.** $x-e$ **45.** n^2-mn

46. $ab+b^2$ **47.** $\dfrac{n-a}{z}$ **48.** $\dfrac{x-z}{p}$ **49.** T^2+t^2 **50.** $\dfrac{C}{dn}$

Exercise 13   _page 86_

1. $\dfrac{9}{2}$ **2.** 7 **3.** $\dfrac{t-b}{n}$ **4.** $\dfrac{q-v}{m}$ **5.** $\dfrac{B+A}{p}$

6. $\dfrac{A+q}{n}$ **7.** $\dfrac{n^2+w}{k}$ **8.** $\dfrac{n-m}{m}$ **9.** $\dfrac{e-m}{t}$ **10.** $\dfrac{v^2+w^2}{B}$

11. $\dfrac{d-L}{p}$ **12.** $\dfrac{M+n}{m}$ **13.** $\dfrac{x-y}{x}$ **14.** $\dfrac{v^2+t}{x}$ **15.** $\dfrac{z^2+s^2}{s}$

16. $\dfrac{x^2-pq}{r}$ **17.** $\dfrac{h^2-lm}{b}$ **18.** $\dfrac{d+b-t}{e}$ **19.** $\dfrac{p^2-m-n}{B}$ **20.** $\dfrac{km+n^2}{m}$

21. $\dfrac{t+mn}{m}$ **22.** $\dfrac{x-ux}{u}$ **23.** $\dfrac{y-pw}{p}$ **24.** $\dfrac{q+Au}{A}$ **25.** $\dfrac{m-Lx}{L}$

26. $\dfrac{x^3-nx^2}{n}$ **27.** $\dfrac{s^2+r^2}{r}$ **28.** $\dfrac{y^2+x^2}{x}$ **29.** $\dfrac{13}{3}$ **30.** $-\dfrac{2}{5}$

31. $\dfrac{T+nt}{n}$ **32.** $\dfrac{V+wy}{w}$ **33.** $\dfrac{w+q+mw}{m}$ **34.** $\dfrac{x^2-y^2+z^2}{z}$ **35.** $\dfrac{v^2-ut}{t}$

36. $\dfrac{L^2-MN}{m}$ **37.** $\dfrac{x-zx}{z}$ **38.** $\dfrac{y^2+w^2}{w}$ **39.** $\dfrac{x^2+2q^2}{q}$ **40.** $\dfrac{n}{k}$

Exercise 14   _page 86_

1. an **2.** At **3.** x^2 **4.** zp **5.** vw
6. n^3 **7.** $-em$ **8.** $t(a-b)$ **9.** $h(x+y)$ **10.** $-m^2$

11. $z(a+b)$ **12.** $B(m-n)$ **13.** $D(m-p)$ **14.** $\dfrac{an}{m}$ **15.** $\dfrac{yx}{n}$

16. $\dfrac{ey}{a}$ **17.** $\dfrac{az}{v}$ **18.** $\dfrac{a^2}{m}$ **19.** $\dfrac{xy}{z}$ **20.** $\dfrac{vw}{q}$

21. $\dfrac{bx}{am}$ **22.** $\dfrac{Ac}{mx}$ **23.** $\dfrac{v^2}{bz}$ **24.** $\dfrac{t^2}{en}$ **25.** $\dfrac{a(x+y)}{m}$

26. $\dfrac{d(p+q)}{n}$ **27.** $\dfrac{q(x+t)}{A}$ **28.** $\dfrac{n}{a+d^2}$ **29.** $\dfrac{w^2}{B^2}$ **30.** $\dfrac{v^2}{z^2}$

THINK ABOUT IT   2

Exercise A   *page 89*

1. 230   **2.** (a) £30   (b) 2400 g   **3.** (a) 52 m^2 (b) 0.052 m^3 **4.** 500
5. (b) 0.2   (c) $\frac{1}{2}$ (d) 0.75   (e) $\frac{3}{5}$ (f) 0.625   **6.** £12.60
7. (a) 14.52   (b) 0.648   (c) 13.4   (d) 18.05   (e) 2.56   (f) 35.1   **8.** £760
9. pencils by 10p   **10.** (a) 6, 8, 54   (b) 6, 15, 27, 39, 54   (c) 7, 13, 17, 23, 41   (d) 27, 54

Project 2   *page 90*

1. SOIL	**2.** ISLES	**3.** HE LIES	**4.** SOS
5. HO HO HO	**6.** ESSO OIL	**7.** SOLID	**8.** SOLO
9. BOILED EGGS	**10.** HE IS BOSS	**11.** LODGE	**12.** SIGH
13. HEDGEHOG	**14.** GOSH	**15.** GOBBLE	**16.** BEG
17. BIG SLOB	**18.** SID	**19.** HILL	**20.** LESLIE
21. HOBBIES	**22.** GIGGLE	**23.** BIBLE	**24.** BIGGLES
25. BOBBLE	**26.** HEIDI	**27.** BOBBIE	**28.** HIGH
29. HELLS BELLS	**30.** GOD BLESS	**31.** SHE DIES	**32.** SOLEIL

Exercise B   *page 91*

1. 10   **2.** (a) £6.54   (b) £15.71   (c) £11.62   (d) £8.03   (e) £0.63   (f) £1.07
3. 20   **4.** (a) 60 cm^2 (b) 24 cm^2 (c) 40%   **5.** (a) £1920   (b) £6580
6. 270   **7.** £7.12   **8.** (a) 410   (b) 704.5
9. (a) 64   (b) 1   (c) 100   (d) 3000   (e) 32   (f) 81   **10.** 20 cm^2

Exercise C   *page 92*

1.

9	+	6	→	15
×		÷		
4	+	2	→	6
↓		↓		
36	÷	3	→	12

2.

8	+	3	→	11
−		×		
3	×	1	→	3
↓		↓		
5	+	3	→	8

3.

15	+	19	→	34
×		+		
5	×	31	→	155
↓		↓		
75	+	50	→	125

4.

38	+	14	→	52
×		+		
3	÷	1	→	3
↓		↓		
114	−	15	→	99

5.

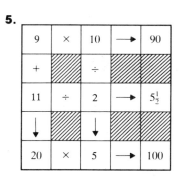

9	×	10	→	90
+		÷		
11	÷	2	→	$5\frac{1}{2}$
↓		↓		
20	×	5	→	100

6.

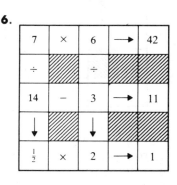

7	×	6	→	42
÷		÷		
14	−	3	→	11
↓		↓		
$\frac{1}{2}$	×	2	→	1

7.

17	×	2	→	34
−		÷		
9	×	4	→	36
↓		↓		
8	−	$\frac{1}{2}$	→	$7\frac{1}{2}$

8.

90	−	7	→	83
÷		×		
2	÷	8	→	$\frac{1}{4}$
↓		↓		
45	+	56	→	101

9.

9	×	5	→	45
×		−		
1	×	2	→	2
↓		↓		
9	×	3	→	27

10.

25	×	10	→	250
−		÷		
16	÷	100	→	0.16
↓		↓		
9	−	0·1	→	8.9

11.

0·1	×	20	→	2
×		+		
6	−	0.2	→	5.8
↓		↓		
0·6	+	20.2	→	20·8

12.

$\frac{1}{2}$	×	100	→	50
−		×		
0.1	+	2	→	2·1
↓		↓		
0·4	×	200	→	80

13.

7	×	0·1	→	0·7
÷		×		
5	÷	0·2	→	10
↓		↓		
1.4	+	0.02	→	1.42

14.

1.2	+	6	→	7·2
+		×		
7	÷	5	→	1.4
↓		↓		
8·2	+	30	→	38·2

15.

100	×	0.2	→	20
−		×		
1.2	+	10	→	11·2
↓		↓		
98·8	+	2	→	100.8

16.

4	×	$\frac{1}{2}$	→	2
÷×		+		
1	−	$\frac{1}{4}$	→	$\frac{3}{4}$
↓		↓		
4	×	$\frac{3}{4}$	→	3

17.

$\frac{1}{4}$	−	$\frac{1}{8}$	→	$\frac{1}{8}$
×		×		
$\frac{1}{2}$	÷	4	→	$\frac{1}{8}$
↓		↓		
$\frac{1}{8}$	+	$\frac{1}{2}$	→	$\frac{5}{8}$

18.

0·4	−	0·01	→	0.39
+		×		
3.6	×	10	→	36
↓		↓		
4	÷	0·1	→	40

Exercise D   *page 95*

1. £0.78; £1.80; 7; £14.63   **2.** £6.30   **3.** 52 cm^2

4. 1, 10, 5, 48   **5.** (a) 214 500   (b) 580   **6.** (a) 0.4 km   (b) 2 cm   **7.** 6 years

8. $7\frac{7}{8}$ **9.** (a) $144 + 538 = 682$ (b) $837 - 356 = 481$ **10.** 9

Project 6   *page 98*

1. (a) Sally   (b) John, Dave   (c) Dave   (d) 7   **2.** (a) 4   (b) 9
3. (a) 19   (b) 22   (c) 31   (d) 42   **4.** $m = p - 1$

Exercise F   *page 100*

1. (a) £162   (b) 200   (c) F1000   (d) £100
2. (a) £114.80   (b) £12   (c) 224 tiles
3. (a) £4.04   (b) £55.60   (c) (i) £445.20   (ii) £45.20   (d) (i) £891.12   (ii) £161.12

Project 7   *page 101*

Number	3	5	13	11	14	17	32	19	23	33	39
Number of steps to reach 1	7	5	9	14	17	12	5	20	15	26	34

Exercise G   *page 101*

1. (a) 1440   (b) 18 720 km   (c) £982.50   (d) £1017.90
2. (a) £64   (b) £326.40   (c) £390.40   (d) £294.40
3. (a) £560   (b) £46.67   **4.** 15   **5.** (f) 1089

PART 7

Exercise 1   *page 104*

1. 70°   **2.** 100°   **3.** 70°   **4.** 100°
5. 55°   **6.** 70°   **7.** 70°   **8.** $33\frac{1}{3}°$
9. 30°   **10.** 35°   **11.** 155°   **12.** 125°
13. 44°   **14.** 80°   **15.** 40°   **16.** 48°
17. 40°   **18.** 35°   **19.** $a = 40°, b = 140°$ **20.** $x = 108°, y = 72°$

Exercise 2   *page 105*

1. 50°   **2.** 70°   **3.** 130°   **4.** 73°
5. 18°   **6.** 75°   **7.** 29°   **8.** 30°
9. 70°   **10.** 42°   **11.** 120°   **12.** 100°
13. 45°   **14.** 72°   **15.** 40°   **16.** $a = 55°, b = 70°$
17. $c = 72°, d = 36°$ **18.** $w = 55°, z = 55°$ **19.** 80°   **20.** 75°
21. 60°   **22.** $x = 122°, y = 116°$ **23.** 135°   **24.** 30°
25. 65°   **26.** $a = 154°, b = 52°$

Exercise 3   *page 107*

1. 72°   **2.** 98°   **3.** 80°   **4.** 74°
5. 86°   **6.** 88°   **7.** $x = 95°, y = 50°$ **8.** $a = 87°, b = 74°$
9. $a = 65°, c = 103°$ **10.** $a = 68°, b = 42°$ **11.** $y = 65°, z = 50°$ **12.** $a = 55°, b = 75°, c = 50°$

Exercise 4   *page 108*

1. 42°   **2.** 68°   **3.** 100°   **4.** 73°
5. 50°   **6.** 52°   **7.** 84°   **8.** $a = 70°, b = 60°$
9. $x = 58°, y = 109°$ **10.** 66°   **11.** 65°   **12.** $e = 70°, f = 30°$
13. $x = 72°, y = 36°$ **14.** $a = 68°, b = 72°, c = 68°$ **15.** 4°   **16.** $28\frac{1}{2}°$
17. 20°   **18.** $x = 62°, y = 28°$ **19.** 34°   **20.** 58°

Test 1   *page 109*

1. 99	**2.** 20	**3.** 600	**4.** 204 020	**5.** 9 o'clock
6. 310	**7.** 30	**8.** £6.80	**9.** £1.80	**10.** 20p, 20p, 2p, 2p
11. 0.5	**12.** 4	**13.** Tuesday	**14.** 160 cm	**15.** £2.07
16. 64 cm	**17.** £212	**18.** £2000	**19.** 8	**20.** 57
21. 36	**22.** 20	**23.** 82	**24.** £5	**25.** £1.32
26. £4.64	**27.** £2.60	**28.** 50	**29.** 300	**30.** 20p

Test 2   *page 109*

1. £47	**2.** 0.25	**3.** 9	**4.** 166	**5.** £12
6. £15	**7.** 10, 10, 5, 5	**8.** 92	**9.** 67 cm	**10.** £8.50
11. 4	**12.** 9.10	**13.** Sunday	**14.** 8	**15.** 54
16. 14	**17.** 510 280	**18.** 200	**19.** 51 cm	**20.** 20
21. 18	**22.** 54	**23.** £4.14	**24.** 90	**25.** £7.20
26. 195	**27.** £1000	**28.** 140	**29.** £1.80	**30.** 17th January

Test 3   *page 110*

1. 63p	**2.** 51	**3.** £10	**4.** 4	**5.** 36
6. Monday	**7.** 12 ounces	**8.** 7.25	**9.** 5, 5, 5, 5	**10.** 0.3
11. 250	**12.** 270 cm	**13.** 25	**14.** 200	**15.** 3
16. 17 009	**17.** 3	**18.** £3140	**19.** 45	**20.** 4
21. 50	**22.** 20 cm	**23.** 79	**24.** £9.78	**25.** £1.20
26. £4.80	**27.** 77	**28.** £30	**29.** 43	**30.** 450

Test 4   *page 111*

1. 59	**2.** 9	**3.** £4.25	**4.** 118
5. 50, 20, 5, 2	**6.** 84p	**7.** 20 past 10 (10.20)	**8.** Sunday
9. 0.2	**10.** 0.75	**11.** 24	**12.** 200
13. 4	**14.** 230	**15.** 8	**16.** £32
17. 34	**18.** 4	**19.** 91	**20.** 34
21. 76	**22.** 16	**23.** 180 cm	**24.** 3000
25. £3.28	**26.** 230	**27.** £2	**28.** 144
29. £7.20	**30.** £8.05		

Test 5   *page 111*

1. 20	**2.** 39	**3.** 5	**4.** 0.2	**5.** 120
6. 6 gallons	**7.** £2.40	**8.** 3	**9.** 426 g	**10.** $7\frac{1}{2}$
11. 15	**12.** 20	**13.** 320	**14.** 50, 5, 5, 5 or 20, 20, 20, 5	
15. 75%	**16.** £18.50	**17.** 180	**18.** 202 004	**19.** 0.03
20. £9.36	**21.** 04 30	**22.** £10	**23.** £2.30	**24.** 8
25. £1.08	**26.** 0.3	**27.** 43	**28.** £2.80	**29.** 62 m.p.h.
30. see Qu. **14**				

Test 6   *page 112*

1. 84	**2.** £2.60	**3.** $\frac{1}{2}$	**4.** 12	**5.** 20
6. 180°	**7.** 952	**8.** $11\frac{1}{2}$	**9.** 20 000	**10.** $\frac{1}{100}$
11. £1.70	**12.** 350	**13.** 120	**14.** 2	**15.** 20
16. 207 820	**17.** 60	**18.** 5 or 31	**19.** £1.60	**20.** 10 cm
21. 5	**22.** £70	**23.** £14	**24.** £2.50	**25.** £39
26. 6	**27.** £10	**28.** 13	**29.** 1 hr 45 min	**30.** 75%

Exercise 24   *page 12*

1. 5.5×10^3	**2.** 6.14×10^4	**3.** 2.3×10^7	**4.** 1.7×10^6
5. 8.45×10^5	**6.** 2.71×10^4	**7.** 6×10^9	**8.** 8.1×10^9
9. 7.4×10^6	**10.** 8.96×10^6	**11.** 7.14×10^3	**12.** 6.6×10^4
13. 8.4×10^6	**14.** 7.46×10^5	**15.** 2×10^2	**16.** 4.4×10^3
17. 7.5×10^1	**18.** 8.26×10^8	**19.** 2×10^6	**20.** 3×10^7
21. 4.6×10^{-4}	**22.** 2.3×10^{-5}	**23.** 4.1×10^{-3}	**24.** 7.58×10^{-8}
25. 8.23×10^{-2}	**26.** 9.58×10^{-5}	**27.** 6.15×10^{-6}	**28.** 1.52×10^{-6}
29. 7.56×10^{-2}	**30.** 6.164×10^{-3}	**31.** 8.8×10^{-6}	**32.** 8.14×10^{-3}
33. 9.5×10^{-9}	**34.** 7.4×10^{-2}	**35.** 8×10^{-2}	**36.** 9.5×10^{-1}
37. 7.14×10^{-4}	**38.** 9.99×10^{-1}	**39.** 8.415×10^{-2}	**40.** 4.5×10^{-5}

Exercise 25   *page 12*

1. 230	**2.** 340 000	**3.** 4100	**4.** 271	**5.** 82 000
6. 300 000 000	**7.** 900	**8.** 220 000	**9.** 63.5	**10.** 89 500
11. 400 000	**12.** 1234	**13.** 514	**14.** 80	**15.** 7000
16. 605	**17.** 80 120	**18.** 60 000 000	**19.** 960	**20.** 42 000
21. 0.042	**22.** 0.004 7	**23.** 0.001 6	**24.** 0.000 89	**25.** 0.84
26. 0.06	**27.** 0.000 951	**28.** 0.000 02	**29.** 0.000 08	**30.** 0.41
31. 0.006 3	**32.** 0.008 04	**33.** 0.05	**34.** 0.069	**35.** 0.000 48
36. 0.895	**37.** 0.061 1	**38.** 0.000 000 8	**39.** 0.000 009	**40.** 0.001 11
41. 5200	**42.** 0.009 4	**43.** 0.08	**44.** 380 000	**45.** 0.000 67
46. 0.066 6	**47.** 11 000	**48.** 0.008 1	**49.** 0.7	**50.** 5 000 000

PART 2

Exercise 1   *page 13*

1. 3.6	**2.** 8.5	**3.** 47	**4.** 9.6	**5.** 56
6. 740	**7.** 2300	**8.** 1152	**9.** 80	**10.** 65 400
11. 0.0075	**12.** 0.0815	**13.** 0.000 047	**14.** 0.62	**15.** 0.005 2
16. 0.31	**17.** 0.163	**18.** 0.07	**19.** 0.007 2	**20.** 0.045
21. 470	**22.** 622	**23.** 8.26	**24.** 0.0858	**25.** 0.07
26. 0.007 3	**27.** 0.573	**28.** 1450	**29.** 0.0264	**30.** 60 000
31. 6	**32.** 0.000 006	**33.** 400	**34.** 0.015	**35.** 8.5
36. 8000	**37.** 6 300 000	**38.** 0.006	**39.** 0.849	**40.** 600

Exercise 2   *page 14*

1. 0.85 m	**2.** 2400 m	**3.** 63 cm	**4.** 0.25 m	**5.** 0.7 cm
6. 20 mm	**7.** 1200 m	**8.** 700 cm	**9.** 580 m	**10.** 0.815 m
11. 0.65 km	**12.** 2.5 cm	**13.** 5000 g	**14.** 4200 g	**15.** 6400 g
16. 3000 g	**17.** 800 g	**18.** 0.4 kg	**19.** 2000 kg	**20.** 0.25 kg
21. 500 kg	**22.** 620 kg	**23.** 0.007 t	**24.** 1.5 kg	**25.** 0.8 l
26. 2000 ml	**27.** 1 l	**28.** 4500 ml	**29.** 6000 ml	**30.** 3000 cm^3
31. 2000 l	**32.** 5500 l	**33.** 900 cm^3	**34.** 0.6 l	**35.** 15 000 l
36. 0.24 l	**37.** 0.28 m	**38.** 550 cm	**39.** 0.305 kg	**40.** 46 m
41. 0.016 l	**42.** 0.208 m	**43.** 2.8 cm	**44.** 0.27 m	**45.** 0.788 km
46. 14 000 kg	**47.** 1300 g	**48.** 0.09 m^3	**49.** 2900 kg	**50.** 0.019 l

Exercise 3   *page 14*

1. 24	**2.** 48	**3.** 30	**4.** 4480	**5.** 48	**6.** 17 600
7. 36	**8.** 70	**9.** 4	**10.** 880	**11.** 3	**12.** 2

13. 3520	**14.** 80	**15.** 140	**16.** 12	**17.** 48	**18.** 22 400
19. 5280	**20.** 2	**21.** 30	**22.** 62	**23.** 76	**24.** 101
25. 18	**26.** 8	**27.** 58	**28.** 92	**29.** 4	**30.** 152

Exercise 4   *page 15*

1. 25.4 cm	**2.** 16.1 km	**3.** 4.4 lb	**4.** 1.242 miles	**5.** 45.5 litres
6. 2.2 gallons	**7.** 11 lb	**8.** 62.1 miles	**9.** 15.24 cm	**10.** 6.44 km
11. 36.4 litres	**12.** 2.272 litres	**13.** 55 lb	**14.** 1610 km	**15.** 7.452 miles
16. 4.54 kg	**17.** 7.62 cm	**18.** 4.4 gallons	**19.** 1.32 gallons	**20.** 4.347 miles

Exercise 5   *page 15*

1. £85 000   **2.** 2128   **3.** £17.55   **4.** (a) $72.50   (b) $0.87   **5.** 302
6. £2063.58   **7.** £14.08
8. (a) 24, 29   (b) 30, 20   (c) 8, 2   (d) 2, $\frac{2}{3}$ **9.** £2.05   **10.** 2h 55 min

Exercise 6   *page 16*

1. £900   **2.** £84   **3.** 49 747   **4.** 6   **5.** 13 950   **6.** £12.50
7. £3515   **8.** £120   **9.** (a) $6400   (b) $83 200   **10.** £1.80

Exercise 7   *page 16*

1. £43   **2.** 552   **3.** (a) double 18   (b) £11,111   **4.** 50
5. (a) £360   (b) £225   (c) £3.75
6. (a) 9, 21, 33, 39   (b) 5, 11   (c) 38   (d) 21
7. (a) 7.2   (b) 11.28   (c) 0.1   (d) 0.026   (e) 28.2   (f) 0.01
8. (a) 3.32   (b) 1.61   (c) 1.46   (d) 4.4   (e) 6.2   (f) 2.74
9. (a) 8   (b) 24   **10.** £345

Exercise 8   *page 17*

1. 73   **2.** £63   **3.** (a) 680   (b) 13 600   **4.** 140
5. (a) $\frac{1}{10}$ (b) $\frac{1}{20}$ (c) $\frac{1}{2}$ (d) $\frac{3}{4}$ **6.** (a) 49   (b) 1   (c) 81   (d) 13   (e) 125
    (f) 28   **7.** 37   **8.** (a) 30   (b) 45   (c) 48   **9.** A = 4, B = 1, C = 8
10. (a) 6, 5   (b) 12, 3   (c) 9, 4

Exercise 9   *page 17*

1. 42 kg   **2.** 360 000 kg   **3.** (a) 600   (b) £204   **4.** £15
5. (a) 07 30   (b) 19 30   (c) 13 00   **6.** 12   **7.** 120   **8.** 72 m.p.h.
9. (b) (i) 7 miles   (ii) 10 miles   (iii) 8 miles   (iv) 7 miles   (v) 14 miles   (vi) 9 miles
10. 11

Exercise 10   *page 18*

1. 20   **2.** 37   **3.** 10% of £600 is greater by £7.50   **4.** (a) 16 m^2 (b) 6 m^3
5. (a) 50, 20, 5, 2   (b) 50, 20, 10, 5, 1   (c) £1, 50, 5, 1, 1   **6.** 817, 8117, 8171, 8710, 8711
7. £77.91   **8.** 480
9. (a) 52 g   (b) 35p   (c) 15   **10.** (a) 3, 4   (b) 5, 2   (c) 7, 4

Exercise 11   *page 18*

1. 6   **2.** £166   **3.** 150 g
4. (a) £41.20   (b) £8.20   (c) £32.88   (d) £27.16
5. 48 cm^2 **6.** 5 cm   **7.** Steven 30, Peter 20
8. (a) 110   (b) 165   (c) 150   (d) 240
9. m, 9, z

10. (a)   (b)   (c)

Exercise 12   *page 19*

1. (a) 31p   (b) 6   **2.** 2016, 2061, 2106, 2601, 2616   **3.** £8.50
4. (a) 108 m²   (b) 3   **6.** 1.50 m   **7.** 42 km
8. (a) £13.50   (b) £21.60   (c) £11.25   **9.** 78   **10.** £1.70

Exercise 13   *page 20*

1. $42\frac{1}{2}$ h   **2.** 0.009, 0.05, 0.062, 0.14, 0.41
3. (a) 40 acres   (b) 15 acres   (c) 10%, 30%, 37.5%, 22.5%   **4.** 178
5. 104 cm   **6.** 1.2 l   **7.** 1145   **8.** £1.20   **9.** £2660
10. (a) 16   (b) 36   (c) 27   (d) 10 000   (e) 75   (f) 400

Exercise 14   *page 20*

1. 13   **2.** 10   **3.** 4   **4.** 8   **5.** 2   **6.** 2   **7.** 25   **8.** 17
9. 10   **10.** 31   **11.** 16   **12.** 25   **13.** 32   **14.** 16   **15.** 22   **16.** 14
17. 7   **18.** 1   **19.** $5\frac{1}{2}$ **20.** 46   **21.** 30   **22.** 20   **23.** 12   **24.** 16
25. 8   **26.** 11   **27.** 10   **28.** 9   **29.** 2   **30.** 221   **31.** 10   **32.** 38
33. 19   **34.** 11   **35.** 14   **36.** 21   **37.** 18   **38.** 50   **39.** 21   **40.** 14
41. 34   **42.** 66   **43.** 10   **44.** 21   **45.** 2   **46.** 1   **47.** 39   **48.** 24
49. 3   **50.** 2   **51.** 4   **52.** 9   **53.** 14   **54.** 4   **55.** 2   **56.** 3
57. 0   **58.** 0   **59.** 12   **60.** 10   **61.** 19   **62.** 6   **63.** 6   **64.** 8
65. 2   **66.** 53   **67.** 15   **68.** 605   **69.** 0   **70.** 9   **71.** 73   **72.** 8
73. 17   **74.** 4   **75.** 13   **76.** 1   **77.** 10   **78.** 11   **79.** 21   **80.** 4

Exercise 15   *page 21*

1. 19   **2.** 2   **3.** 30   **4.** 43   **5.** 2   **6.** 4   **7.** 14   **8.** 1
9. 4   **10.** 0   **11.** 32   **12.** 35   **13.** 21   **14.** 20   **15.** 31   **16.** 11
17. 55   **18.** 28   **19.** 0   **20.** 33   **21.** 32   **22.** 79   **23.** 11   **24.** 14
25. 21   **26.** 83   **27.** 56   **28.** 3   **29.** 9   **30.** 35   **31.** 50   **32.** 17
33. 24   **34.** 22   **35.** 32   **36.** 14   **37.** 30   **38.** 14   **39.** 21   **40.** 1
41. 10   **42.** 10   **43.** $9\frac{3}{4}$ **44.** 8   **45.** 22   **46.** 2   **47.** 23   **48.** 8
49. 13   **50.** 2   **51.** 9   **52.** 0   **53.** 11   **54.** 18   **55.** 22   **56.** 19
57. 20   **58.** 15   **59.** 12   **60.** 39   **61.** 13   **62.** 5   **63.** 4   **64.** 20
65. 26   **66.** 5

Exercise 16   *page 22*

1. $7 + 5 \times 4$ **2.** $3 \times 5 + 10$ **3.** $4 \div 2 + 3$ **4.** $11 + 3 \times 3$
5. $31 - 10 \times 2$ **6.** $10 + 6 \times 5$ **7.** $4 \times 8 - 7$ **8.** $12 + 9 \times 2$
9. $18 - 4 \times 4$ **10.** $28 - 10 \times 2$ **11.** $21 \div 3 - 5$ **12.** $7 + 3 \times 3$
13. $10 \div 2 + 3$ **14.** $10 \times 3 + 12$ **15.** $18 \div 3 + 7$ **16.** $31 + 40 \div 5$
17. $15 - 16 \div 4$ **18.** $15 + 8 \times 9$ **19.** $37 + 35 \div 5$ **20.** $11 \times 5 + 9$
21. $8 + 3 \times 2 - 4$ **22.** $12 - 3 \times 3 + 1$ **23.** $11 + 4 - 1 \times 6$ **24.** $15 \div 5 + 2 \times 4$
25. $7 \times 2 - 3 \times 3$ **26.** $12 - 2 + 3 \times 4$ **27.** $8 \times 9 - 6 \times 11$ **28.** $20 \div 20 + 9 \times 0$
29. $20 - 30 \div 10 + 8$ **30.** $30 + 6 \times 11 - 11$

Exercise 17   *page 22*

1. 8%	**2.** 10%	**3.** 25%	**4.** 2%	**5.** 4%	**6.** $2\frac{1}{2}$%
7. 20%	**8.** 50%	**9.** 15%	**10.** 80%	**11.** 20%	**12.** $33\frac{1}{3}$%
13. $12\frac{1}{2}$%	**14.** 10%	**15.** 5%	**16.** 25%	**17.** 20%	**18.** $12\frac{1}{2}$%
19. $33\frac{1}{3}$%	**20.** 80%	**21.** 5%	**22.** 6%	**23.** 20%	**24.** 5%
25. $2\frac{1}{2}$%					

Exercise 18   *page 23*

1. 36.4%	**2.** 19.1%	**3.** 19.4%	**4.** 22.0%	**5.** 12.2%	**6.** 9.4%
7. 14.0%	**8.** 17.4%	**9.** 32.7%	**10.** 10.2%	**11.** 7.7%	**12.** 35.3%
13. 30.8%	**14.** 5.2%	**15.** 14.1%	**16.** 14.5%	**17.** 19.1%	**18.** 3.6%
19. 31.1%	**20.** 6.5%				

Exercise 19   *page 23*

1. 12%	**2.** 29%	**3.** 16%	**4.** 0.25%	**5.** 15%	**6.** 61.1%
7. 15%	**8.** 14.2%	**9.** 1.5%	**10.** 23.8%		

Exercise 20   *page 23*

1. (a) 25p   (b) £12.80   (c) £2.80   (d) 28%
2. (a) £10   (b) (i) £3.50   (ii) 35%   **3.** (a) £10   (b) (i) £4.20   (ii) 42%
4. (a) 25%   (b) (i) £135   (ii) 12.5%
5. (a) (i) 120 cm   (ii) 75 cm   (iii) 10 000 cm^2 (iv) 9000 cm^2 (b) 10%
6. (a) (i) 58 cm   (ii) 30 cm   (iii) 2500 cm^2 (iv) 1740 cm^2 (b) 30.4%
7. (a) £75   (b) (i) £67.50   (ii) 12.5%   **8.** (a) £50 000   (b) (i) £53 800   (ii) 7.6%

Exercise 21   *page 25*

1. (a) 45   (b) 30   (c) 30   (d) 20   **2.** 2 h 10 min   **3.** 2005
4. 'The London Blackout Murders'   **5.** 15 min   **6.** 225 min ($=3\frac{3}{4}$ h)   **7.** 11 h 5 min
8. 21 10   **9.** 5   **10.** 1h 45 min   **11.** 18 00
12. 15 min   **13.** 15 h 10 min

Exercise 22   *page 26*

1. 1939	**2.** 2057	**3.** 2003	**4.** 1914
5. 2057	**6.** 1904	**7.** 2033	**8.** 2037
9. 1957	**10.** 2038	**11.** Northwood Hills	**12.** Watford
13. Croxley	**14.** Moor Park	**15.** Aylesbury	**16.** Finchley Road
17. Harrow-on-the-Hill	**18.** North Harrow	**19.** Preston Road	**20.** Marylebone

Exercise 23   *page 27*

1. 43 min	**2.** 38 min	**3.** 12 min	**4.** 8 min	**5.** 2003	**6.** 2042
7. 2005	**8.** 1905	**9.** 2010	**10.** 1933	**11.** 1945	**12.** 1918
13. 2039	**14.** 1931				

PART 3

Exercise 1   *page 29*

1. 32 cm^2	**2.** 21 cm^2	**3.** 20 cm^2	**4.** 13.5 cm^2	**5.** 14 cm^2
6. 19 cm^2	**7.** 36 m^2	**8.** 130 m^2	**9.** 28 m^2	**10.** 18 cm^2
11. 42 cm^2	**12.** 21 cm^2	**13.** 55 cm^2	**14.** 39 cm^2	**15.** 52 sq. units
16. $35\frac{1}{2}$ sq. units	**17.** 35 sq. units	**18.** $48\frac{1}{2}$ sq. units		

53

Exercise 2   *page 30*

1. 18.8 cm, 28.3 cm^2 2. 31.4 cm, 78.5 cm^2 3. 25.1 cm, 50.3 cm^2
4. 12.6 cm, 12.6 cm^2 5. 28.3 m, 63.6 m^2 6. 9.42 cm, 7.07 cm^2
7. 37.7 m, 113 m^2 8. 34.6 m, 95.0 m^2 9. 26.4 cm, 55.4 cm^2
10. 11.0 m, 9.62 m^2 11. 5.65 cm, 2.54 cm^2 12. 35.2 cm, 98.5 cm^2
13. 5.34 cm, 2.27 cm^2 14. 22.0 feet, 38.5 sq feet   15. 10.1 km, 8.04 km^2
16. 63.5 km, 320 km^2 17. 3.14 mm, 0.785 mm^2 18. 1.57 miles, 0.196 sq. miles
19. 39.6 km, 125 km^2 20. 4.71 miles, 1.77 sq. miles

Exercise 3   *page 31*

1. 36.0 cm, 77.0 cm^2 2. 28.3 cm, 47.5 cm^2 3. 25.7 cm, 39.3 cm^2
4. 28.6 cm, 57.1 cm^2 5. 36.8 cm, 92.5 cm^2 6. 10.7 cm, 7.07 cm^2
7. 7.14 cm, 3.14 cm^2 8. 51.4 cm, 157 cm^2 9. 46.0 cm, 147 cm^2
10. 37.7 cm, 99.3 cm^2 11. 20.6 cm, 24.6 cm^2 12. 20.3 cm, 24.6 cm^2
13. 27.9 cm, 44.6 cm^2

Exercise 4   *page 32*

1. 22.9 cm^2 2. 35.9 cm^2 3. 13.7 cm^2 4. 370 cm^2 5. 21.5 cm^2 6. 84.1 cm^2
7. 24.8 cm^2 8. 25.1 cm^2

Exercise 5   *page 33*

1. 2.39 cm   2. 4.46 m   3. 1.11 m   4. 6.37 cm   5. 4.15 cm   6. 3.48 cm
7. 3.95 m   8. 2.99 m   9. 2.55 m   10. 4.37 cm   11. 4.62 cm   12. 5.57 m
13. 5.75 cm   14. 4.72 cm   15. 3.50 m   16. 8.91 cm   17. 4.07 m   18. 3.74 cm
19. 2.86 m   20. 3.98 cm   21. 3.09 cm   22. 4.77 cm   23. 4.51 m   24. 5.05 cm
25. 5.25 m

Exercise 6   *page 33*

1. 215 m^2 2. 97.5 cm^2 3. 27.7 cm   4. 19.1 m   5. 183 cm^2 6. 35.4 cm
7. 32.9 m   8. 15.6 m^2 9. 30.1 m   10. 49.7 m^2 11. 296 cm^2 12. 22.4 cm
13. 127 cm^2 14. 20.2 m   15. 172 cm^2 16. 12.6 cm^2

Exercise 7   *page 33*

1. 9 cm   2. 7.5 cm   3. 40 cm^2 4. 45 cm^2 5. 31 cm   6. 48 cm
7. (a) 20 sq. units   (b) 10 sq. units   8. 3×4, 6×2, 1×12 9. (a) 0.72 m^2 (b) 1.08 m^2
10. (a) 400 m   (b) 6.3 m   11. (a) $\frac{1}{3}$ (b) $\frac{4}{9}$ (c) 25 cm^2
12. (a) 20 m   (b) 200 m^2 (c) 39.3 m^2 (d) 40 m^2 (e) 37.7 m^2 (f) 117.7 m^2
13. 3.43 m^2 14. 212   15. 272   16. 15   17. 4.55 m   18. 0.637 m

Exercise 8   *page 35*

1. (a) 30 cm^3 (b) 168 cm^3 2. (a) 2.5 cm   (b) 3.25 cm
3. (a) 18 cm^3 (b) 14 cm^3 (c) 170 cm^3 (d) 5 cm   (e) 6 cm
    (f) 1.5 cm   (g) 3.5 cm   (h) 11 cm   (i) 0.2 cm   (j) 2.25 cm
    (k) 0.1 cm   (l) 2.4 cm   (m) 8.5 cm   (n) 7.1 cm
4. 40   5. 100   6. 900

Exercise 9   *page 36*

1. 33.5 cm^3 2. 226 cm^3 3. 101 cm^3 4. 137 cm^3 5. 183 cm^3 6. 603 cm^3
7. 66.0 cm^3 8. 38.8 cm^3 9. 5.70 cm^3 10. 16.8 cm^3 11. 5.75 cm^3 12. 1.53 cm^3
13. 60 cm^3 14. 30 cm^3 15. 14.7 cm^3 16. 207 cm^3

Exercise 10   *page 37*

1. 113 l   **2.** 69.1 l   **3.** B
4. (a) (i) 1920 cm³   (ii) 4800 cm³   (b) (i) £2.25   (ii) giant   (iii) 20p   **5.** 740 cm³
6. (a) 33.5 cm³   (b) 0.628 cm³   (c) 53   **7.** 262 sec (4 min 22 s)
8. (a) 141 cm³   (b) 9.42 cm³   **9.** (a) 79.6 cm³   (b) 637 g

Exercise 11   *page 38*

1. (a) 6   (b) 12   (c) 8   (d) 1
2. (a) 24, 24, 8, 8   (b) 22, 24, 8, 6   (c) 38, 32, 8, 12   (d) 8, 14, 10, 2

THINK ABOUT IT   1

Project 1   *page 41*

circle, divide, radius, axis, log, calculate, angle, equal, add, bracket, test, equation, sum, sin, tan, three, multiply, coordinate, parallel, six, pi, four, diameter.

Exercise A   *page 41*

1. 19 35   **2.** £7.93   **3.** £24   **4.** $\frac{3}{10}$ **5.** 63 cm²   **6.** £8
7. £249.60   **8.** 20 m, 50 m², 35 m², 10, £34   **9.** £26.50   **10.** (a) 15051   (b) 110 miles

Exercise B   *page 45*

1. £365   **2.** £115   **3.** 10.15 a.m.   **4.** £7   **5.** x, 5, t **6.** (a) 12   (b) 8, 48
8. 672   **9.** 360 cm³   **10.** 0.006 25 cm

Project 3   *page 45*

Formula is $A = \frac{1}{2}p + i - 1$ [Pick's theorem]

Exercise C   *page 47*

1.

11	+	4	→	15
×		÷		
6	÷	2	→	3
↓		↓		
66	×	2	→	132

2.

9	+	17	→	26
×		−		
5	×	8	→	40
↓		↓		
45	÷	9	→	5

3.

14	+	17	→	31
×		+		
4	×	23	→	92
↓		↓		
56	−	40	→	16

4.

15	÷	3	→	5
+		×		
22	×	5	→	110
↓		↓		
37	−	15	→	22

5.

9	×	10	→	90
+		÷		
11	÷	2	→	5½
↓		↓		
20	×	5	→	100

6.

26	×	2	→	52
−		×		
18	×	4	→	72
↓		↓		
8	÷	8	→	1

7.

5	×	12	→	60
×		÷		
20	+	24	→	44
↓		↓		
100	×	½	→	50

8.

7	×	6	→	42
÷		÷		
14	−	3	→	11
↓		↓		
½	×	2	→	1

9.

19	×	2	→	38
−		÷		
12	×	4	→	48
↓		↓		
7	−	½	→	$6\frac{1}{2}$

10.

17	×	10	→	170
−		÷		
9	÷	100	→	0.09
↓		↓		
8	−	0.1	→	7.9

11.

0·3	×	20	→	6
+		−		
11	÷	11	→	1
↓		↓		
11·3	−	9	→	2·3

12.

½	×	50	→	25
−		÷		
0.1	+	½	→	0·6
↓		↓		
0·4	×	100	→	40

13.

7	×	0.1	→	0·7
÷		×		
4	÷	0.2	→	20
↓		↓		
1·75	+	0·02	→	1.77

14.

1.4	+	8	→	9·4
−		×		
0.1	×	0·1	→	0.01
↓		↓		
1·3	+	0·8	→	2·1

15.

100	×	0.3	→	30
−		×		
2.5	÷	10	→	0·25
↓		↓		
97·5	+	3	→	100.5

16.

3	÷	2	→	1.5
÷		÷		
8	÷	16	→	½
↓		↓		
$\frac{3}{8}$	+	$\frac{1}{8}$	→	½

17.

¼	−	$\frac{1}{16}$	→	$\frac{3}{16}$
×		×		
½	÷	4	→	$\frac{1}{8}$
↓		↓		
$\frac{1}{8}$	+	¼	→	$\frac{3}{8}$

18.

0·5	−	0·01	→	0.49
+		×		
3.5	×	10	→	35
↓		↓		
4	÷	0.1	→	40

Project 4   *page 48*

1. Maths is very hard.
2. One plus one is two.
3. Spurs are rubbish.
4. The earth is round.
5. Can you boil an egg.
6. My teachers are clever.
7. My calculator is wrong.

Exercise D   *page 51*

1. £22.50
2. (a) £58   (b) £62   (c) £125   (d) £7   (e) £11   (f) £568
3. 16.275 kg
4. (a) 30   (b) 200 m^2 5. 3   6. 33
7. (a) £4600   (b) £5400   (c) £8200   8. 2 h 30 min
9. (a) 5000   (b) 40 000   (c) 6000   (d) 100 000   10. $\frac{5}{8} = 0.625$, $\frac{7}{11} = 0.6\dot{3}$

Project 5   *page 51*

$2[5(x + 11) − 7] + 4 = 10x + 100.$

Exercise E   *page 52*

1. $5 \times 999 = 4995$
$6 \times 999 = 5994$
$7 \times 999 = 6993$
$8 \times 999 = 7992$
$9 \times 999 = 8991$

2. $5 + 9 \times 1234 \quad = 11111$
$6 + 9 \times 12345 \quad = 111111$
$7 + 9 \times 123456 \quad = 1111111$
$8 + 9 \times 1234567 \quad = 11111111$
$9 + 9 \times 12345678 = 111111111$

3. $54321 \times 9 - 1 = 488888$
$654321 \times 9 - 1 = 5888888$
$7654321 \times 9 - 1 = 68888888$
$87654321 \times 9 - 1 = 788888888$
$987654321 \times 9 - 1 = 8888888888$

4. (a) $1^3 + 2^3 + 3^3 + \quad 4^3 = (1 + 2 + 3 + 4)^2 = 100$
$1^3 + 2^3 + ... + \quad 5^3 = (1 + 2 + ... + 5)^2 = 225$
$1^3 + 2^3 + ... + \quad 6^3 = (1 + 2 + ... + 6)^2 = 441$
$1^3 + 2^3 + ... + \quad 7^3 = (1 + 2 + ... + 7)^2 = 784$

(b) $1^3 + 2^3 + ... + 10^3 = (1 + 2 + ... + 10)^2 = 3025$

5. (a) $(4.5)^2 = (4 \times 5) + 0.25$
$(5.5)^2 = (5 \times 6) + 0.25$
$(6.5)^2 = (6 \times 7) + 0.25$

(b) $(9.5)^2 = (9 \times 10) + 0.25$
$(15.5)^2 = (15 \times 16) + 0.25$
$(99.5)^2 = (99 \times 100) + 0.25$

6. $13 + 15 + 17 + 19 \qquad\qquad = 64 = 4^3$
$21 + 23 + 25 + 27 + 29 \qquad = 125 = 5^3$
$31 + 33 + 35 + 37 + 39 + 41 \quad = 216 = 6^3$
$43 + 45 + 47 + 49 + 51 + 53 + 55 \quad = 343 = 7^3$
$57 + 59 + 61 + 63 + 65 + 67 + 69 + 71 = 512 = 8^3$

7. (b) $3 \to 14, 4 \to 18, 5 \to 22, 6 \to 26$ (c) (i) 42   (ii) 62   (iii) 202
(d) (i) 12   (ii) 40   (e) $n = 4x + 2$

Exercise F   *page 54*

1. 31576   **2.** 87925   **3.** 47426   **4.** 92474   **5.** 49302   **6.** 14865   **7.** 12218
8. 35752   **9.** 34807

PART 4

Exercise 1   *page 56*

1. -4 **2.** -12 **3.** -11 **4.** -3 **5.** -5 **6.** 4   **7.** -5 **8.** -8
9. 19   **10.** -17 **11.** -4 **12.** -5 **13.** -11 **14.** 6   **15.** -4 **16.** 6
17. 0   **18.** -18 **19.** -3 **20.** -11 **21.** -8 **22.** -7 **23.** 1   **24.** 1
25. 9   **26.** 11   **27.** -8 **28.** 42   **29.** 4   **30.** 15   **31.** -7 **32.** -9
33. -1 **34.** -7 **35.** 0   **36.** 11   **37.** -14 **38.** 0   **39.** 17   **40.** 3

Exercise 2   *page 57*

1. 6   **2.** -32 **3.** -6 **4.** -12 **5.** -16 **6.** 9   **7.** -18
8. -40 **9.** -25 **10.** -800 **11.** -4 **12.** -16 **13.** -8 **14.** 5
15. 2   **16.** -5 **17.** 4   **18.** -5 **19.** -9 **20.** 0   **21.** -1
22. 1   **23.** -400 **24.** -54 **25.** -100 **26.** -5 **27.** 36   **28.** 1
29. 0   **30.** 500

Exercise 3   *page 57*

1. 3, 2   **2.** 2, 4   **3.** 3, 4   **4.** 1, 5   **5.** 2, 6   **6.** 3, 6
7. 2, 7   **8.** 1, 8   **9.** 5, 6   **10.** 2, 15   **11.** 3, 10   **12.** 3, 8
13. 4, 6   **14.** 2, 12   **15.** 1, 24   **16.** 4, 9   **17.** $-1, -2$ **18.** $-3, -2$
19. $-2, -4$ **20.** $-3, -4$ **21.** $-2, -5$ **22.** $-5, -4$ **23.** $-4, -6$ **24.** $-3, -7$
25. $-7, -6$ **26.** $-3, -10$ **27.** 3, -1 **28.** 2, -3 **29.** 3, -2 **30.** 4, -1

31. 1, −4   **32.** 2, −5   **33.** 3, −4   **34.** 6, −1   **35.** 3, −5   **36.** 2, −4
37. 4, 5   **38.** 4, −2   **39.** −4, −1   **40.** 6, −2   **41.** −5, −1   **42.** 7, 3
43. 5, −2   **44.** −6, −2   **45.** −8, −1

Test 1   *page 58*

1. −16   **2.** 64   **3.** −15   **4.** −2   **5.** 15   **6.** 18   **7.** 3   **8.** −6
9. 11   **10.** −48   **11.** −7   **12.** 9   **13.** 6   **14.** −18   **15.** −10   **16.** 8
17. −6   **18.** −30   **19.** 4   **20.** −1

Test 2   *page 58*

1. −16   **2.** 6   **3.** −13   **4.** 42   **5.** −4   **6.** −4   **7.** −12   **8.** −20
9. 6   **10.** 0   **11.** 36   **12.** −10   **13.** −7   **14.** 10   **15.** 6   **16.** −18
17. −9   **18.** 15   **19.** 1   **20.** 0

Test 3   *page 58*

1. 100   **2.** −20   **3.** −8   **4.** −7   **5.** −4   **6.** 10   **7.** 9   **8.** −10
9. 7   **10.** 35   **11.** −20   **12.** −24   **13.** −10   **14.** −7   **15.** −19   **16.** −1
17. −5   **18.** −13   **19.** 0   **20.** 8

Test 4   *page 58*

1. 0   **2.** −16   **3.** −14   **4.** 24   **5.** −1   **6.** 14   **7.** −2   **8.** −2
9. 7   **10.** 33   **11.** −1   **12.** −30   **13.** −28   **14.** 19   **15.** −9   **16.** −8
17. 1   **18.** −9   **19.** −16   **20.** 4

Test 5   *page 58*

1. 7   **2.** −8   **3.** −9   **4.** −22   **5.** 11   **6.** 13   **7.** −2   **8.** −18
9. −6   **10.** 15   **11.** −3   **12.** 0   **13.** 18   **14.** 8   **15.** 2   **16.** 6
17. −5   **18.** −8   **19.** −40   **20.** −3

Test 6   *page 58*

1. −4   **2.** −12   **3.** 50   **4.** −15   **5.** −9   **6.** 14   **7.** 7   **8.** 11
9. 18   **10.** 12   **11.** 16   **12.** −14   **13.** −3   **14.** −1   **15.** −1   **16.** 40
17. 7   **18.** 5   **19.** −9   **20.** −3

Exercise 4   *page 59*

1. 36   **2.** 29   **3.** 8   **4.** 18   **5.** 84   **6.** 2000
7. 165   **8.** $\sqrt{181}$
9. (a) 43   (b) 64   (c) 1   (d) 85
10. (a) 6   (b) −4   (c) −10   (d) 38
11. (a) 14   (b) 52   (c) 2   (d) 310
12. (a) 10   (b) 30   (c) 10   (d) 94
13. (a) 21   (b) 56   **14.** (a) 56   (b) 105   **15.** (a) 180   (b) 39

Exercise 5   *page 59*

1. 7   **2.** 1   **3.** 11   **4.** 5   **5.** 4   **6.** 13   **7.** 23
8. 1   **9.** 19   **10.** 7   **11.** 17   **12.** 30   **13.** 30   **14.** 30
15. 1   **16.** 14   **17.** 41   **18.** 50   **19.** 60   **20.** 50   **21.** 24
22. 72   **23.** 62   **24.** 120   **25.** 40   **26.** 11   **27.** 29   **28.** 303
29. 1200   **30.** 5   **31.** 14   **32.** 3   **33.** 29   **34.** 29   **35.** 6
36. 11   **37.** 5   **38.** 10   **39.** 7   **40.** 27

Exercise 6   *page 60*

1. 3	**2.** 2	**3.** 10	**4.** 0	**5.** 15	**6.** 5	**7.** 7
8. -5	**9.** 12	**10.** 8	**11.** 5	**12.** 12	**13.** 36	**14.** 15
15. 5	**16.** -5	**17.** 9	**18.** 26	**19.** 6	**20.** 22	**21.** 18
22. 24	**23.** 40	**24.** 24	**25.** -14	**26.** 22	**27.** 14	**28.** 243
29. 240	**30.** -2	**31.** 9	**32.** -2	**33.** 25	**34.** 7	**35.** 60
36. 7	**37.** 6	**38.** 68	**39.** 252	**40.** 12		

Exercise 7   *page 60*

1. 1	**2.** 0	**3.** 2	**4.** 1	**5.** 1	**6.** 5	**7.** 3
8. -4	**9.** -4	**10.** 4	**11.** 0	**12.** -1	**13.** 2	**14.** 4
15. 3	**16.** 1	**17.** -2	**18.** 0	**19.** 17	**20.** -5	**21.** -6
22. -4	**23.** 2	**24.** 6	**25.** 4	**26.** -12	**27.** 6	**28.** -6
29. 5	**30.** 2	**31.** -5	**32.** -8	**33.** 12	**34.** -14	**35.** 5
36. 12	**37.** 13	**38.** 5	**39.** 18	**40.** 36	**41.** 12	**42.** 36
43. 5	**44.** 25	**45.** 1	**46.** 9	**47.** 0	**48.** 1	**49.** 5
50. 16						

Exercise 8   *page 60*

1. 1	**2.** 3	**3.** -1	**4.** 1	**5.** -2	**6.** 3	**7.** 7
8. -5	**9.** -5	**10.** 5	**11.** -2	**12.** 0	**13.** 2	**14.** 3
15. 5	**16.** -10	**17.** 2	**18.** -7	**19.** 11	**20.** -5	**21.** -2
22. -4	**23.** 3	**24.** 6	**25.** 12	**26.** -4	**27.** 9	**28.** -25
29. 5	**30.** 4	**31.** -18	**32.** -5	**33.** 10	**34.** -10	**35.** -50
36. 14	**37.** 5	**38.** 25	**39.** 8	**40.** 16	**41.** 3	**42.** 9
43. 45	**44.** 225	**45.** 1	**46.** 16	**47.** 27	**48.** 4	**49.** 27
50. 5						

Exercise 9   *page 60*

1. 12	**2.** 9	**3.** 18	**4.** 4	**5.** 17	**6.** -5	**7.** 6
8. -7	**9.** 4	**10.** 8	**11.** 17	**12.** -5	**13.** 5	**14.** 6
15. 2	**16.** $\frac{4}{5}$	**17.** $2\frac{1}{3}$	**18.** $7\frac{1}{2}$	**19.** $1\frac{5}{6}$	**20.** 0	**21.** $\frac{5}{9}$
22. 1	**23.** $\frac{1}{5}$	**24.** $\frac{2}{7}$	**25.** $\frac{3}{4}$	**26.** $\frac{2}{3}$	**27.** $1\frac{1}{4}$	**28.** $1\frac{1}{5}$
29. $1\frac{5}{9}$	**30.** $\frac{1}{3}$	**31.** $\frac{1}{2}$	**32.** $\frac{1}{10}$	**33.** $-\frac{3}{8}$	**34.** $\frac{9}{50}$	**35.** $\frac{1}{2}$
36. $\frac{3}{5}$	**37.** $-\frac{4}{9}$	**38.** 0	**39.** $4\frac{5}{8}$	**40.** $-1\frac{3}{7}$	**41.** $2\frac{1}{3}$	**42.** $\frac{3}{4}$
43. 1	**44.** $3\frac{3}{5}$	**45.** $\frac{1}{3}$	**46.** $2\frac{1}{14}$	**47.** -1	**48.** $-\frac{5}{6}$	**49.** $8\frac{1}{4}$
50. -55						

Exercise 10   *page 61*

1. $2\frac{3}{4}$	**2.** $1\frac{2}{3}$	**3.** 2	**4.** $\frac{3}{5}$	**5.** $\frac{1}{2}$	**6.** 2	**7.** $5\frac{1}{3}$
8. $1\frac{1}{5}$	**9.** 0	**10.** $\frac{2}{9}$	**11.** $1\frac{1}{2}$	**12.** $\frac{1}{6}$	**13.** $1\frac{1}{3}$	**14.** $\frac{6}{7}$
15. $\frac{4}{7}$	**16.** 7	**17.** $\frac{5}{8}$	**18.** 5	**19.** $\frac{2}{5}$	**20.** $\frac{1}{3}$	**21.** 4
22. -1	**23.** 1	**24.** $\frac{6}{7}$	**25.** $1\frac{1}{4}$	**26.** 1	**27.** $\frac{7}{9}$	**28.** $-1\frac{1}{2}$
29. $\frac{2}{9}$	**30.** $-1\frac{1}{2}$					

Exercise 11   *page 61*

1. 3	**2.** 5	**3.** $10\frac{1}{2}$	**4.** 4	**5.** $\frac{1}{3}$	**6.** $-4\frac{1}{2}$	**7.** $3\frac{1}{3}$
8. $3\frac{1}{2}$	**9.** $3\frac{2}{3}$	**10.** -2	**11.** $-5\frac{1}{2}$	**12.** $4\frac{1}{5}$	**13.** $\frac{3}{7}$	**14.** $\frac{7}{11}$
15. $4\frac{4}{5}$	**16.** $3\frac{7}{8}$	**17.** -3	**18.** 6	**19.** $-\frac{2}{7}$	**20.** $-1\frac{2}{3}$	**21.** $1\frac{7}{10}$

22. $\frac{1}{2}$ **23.** 1   **24.** $\frac{1}{2}$ **25.** $-\frac{1}{2}$ **26.** $1\frac{2}{5}$ **27.** $1\frac{3}{5}$ **28.** 1
29. $1\frac{1}{4}$ **30.** $\frac{5}{11}$

Exercise 12   page 61

1. $\frac{3}{5}$ **2.** $\frac{4}{7}$ **3.** $\frac{11}{12}$ **4.** $\frac{6}{11}$ **5.** $\frac{2}{3}$ **6.** $\frac{5}{9}$ **7.** $\frac{7}{9}$
8. $1\frac{1}{3}$ **9.** $\frac{1}{2}$ **10.** $\frac{2}{3}$ **11.** 3   **12.** $1\frac{1}{2}$ **13.** $1\frac{2}{5}$ **14.** $\frac{4}{13}$
15. $3\frac{1}{3}$ **16.** $\frac{4}{11}$ **17.** $-1\frac{1}{2}$ **18.** -5 **19.** $-\frac{7}{16}$ **20.** $-\frac{1}{2}$ **21.** -10
22. 5   **23.** $\frac{1}{100}$ **24.** $\frac{2}{13}$ **25.** 5   **26.** $1\frac{7}{8}$ **27.** $-\frac{1}{2}$ **28.** 24
29. 15   **30.** -10 **31.** 21   **32.** 21   **33.** $2\frac{2}{3}$ **34.** $4\frac{3}{8}$ **35.** $1\frac{1}{2}$
36. $3\frac{3}{4}$ **37.** $1\frac{1}{3}$ **38.** $3\frac{3}{5}$ **39.** 2   **40.** $\frac{5}{8}$ **41.** $\frac{7}{19}$ **42.** $-\frac{3}{5}$
43. -24 **44.** -70 **45.** $8\frac{1}{4}$ **46.** 220   **47.** -500 **48.** $-\frac{98}{99}$

Exercise 13   page 62

1. $4\frac{1}{2}$ cm   **2.** $3\frac{1}{2}$ cm   **3.** $\frac{1}{2}$ cm   **4.** 4   **5.** $11\frac{1}{2}$ **6.** 11   **7.** 13
8. 15 cm^2 **9.** 10 cm   **10.** 32   **11.** $4\frac{1}{2}$ **12.** 12   **13.** $17\frac{2}{3}$ **14.** $\frac{1}{3}$
15. 5   **16.** 12   **17.** $3\frac{1}{3}$ **18.** $4\frac{2}{3}$ **19.** 55, 56, 57   **20.** 41, 42, 43, 44

Exercise 14   page 63

1. 5   **2.** 2   **3.** 5   **4.** 2   **5.** 4   **6.** 4
7. 3   **8.** 1   **9.** 16   **10.** 25   **11.** 4   **12.** 3
13. 4   **14.** 8   **15.** 499   **16.** 33   **17.** 4   **18.** 3
19. 7   **20.** 3   **21.** 2   **22.** 3   **23.** 4   **24.** 2
25. 4   **26.** 81   **27.** 5   **28.** 6   **29.** 8   **30.** 26
31. 9, 10   **32.** 4, 5   **33.** 1, 2, 3, 4   **34.** 2, 3, 4   **35.** 8, 9, 10   **36.** 2, 3, 4
37. 7, 8, 9, 10   **38.** 11, 12, 13, 14, 15   **39.** 4, 5, 6   **40.** 195, 196, 197, 198, 199, 200

Exercise 15   page 63

1. $e - b$ **2.** $m + t$ **3.** $a + b + f$ **4.** $A + B - h$ **5.** y

6. $b - a$ **7.** $m - k$ **8.** $w + y - v$ **9.** $\dfrac{b}{a}$ **10.** $\dfrac{m}{h}$

11. $\dfrac{a + b}{m}$ **12.** $\dfrac{c - d}{k}$ **13.** $\dfrac{e + n}{v}$ **14.** $\dfrac{y + z}{3}$ **15.** $\dfrac{r}{p}$

16. $\dfrac{h - m}{m}$ **17.** $\dfrac{a - t}{a}$ **18.** $\dfrac{k + e}{m}$ **19.** $\dfrac{m + h}{u}$ **20.** $\dfrac{t - q}{e}$

21. $\dfrac{v^2 + u^2}{k}$ **22.** $\dfrac{s^2 - t^2}{g}$ **23.** $\dfrac{m^2 - k}{a}$ **24.** $\dfrac{m + v}{m}$ **25.** $\dfrac{c - a}{b}$

26. $\dfrac{y - t}{s}$ **27.** $\dfrac{z - y}{c}$ **28.** $\dfrac{a}{h}$ **29.** $\dfrac{2b}{m}$ **30.** $\dfrac{cd - ab}{k}$

31. $\dfrac{c + ab}{a}$ **32.** $\dfrac{e + cd}{c}$ **33.** $\dfrac{n^2 - m^2}{m}$ **34.** $\dfrac{t + ka}{k}$ **35.** $\dfrac{k + h^2}{h}$

36. $\dfrac{n - mb}{m}$ **37.** $2a$ **38.** $\dfrac{d - ac}{c}$ **39.** $\dfrac{e - mb}{m}$ **40.** $\dfrac{t^2 + n^2}{n}$

Exercise 16   *page 64*

1. mt

2. en

3. ap

4. amt

5. abc

6. ey^2

7. $a(b + c)$

8. $t(c - d)$

9. $m(s + t)$

10. $k(h + i)$

11. $\dfrac{ab}{c}$

12. $\dfrac{mz}{y}$

13. $\dfrac{ch}{d}$

14. $\dfrac{em}{k}$

15. $\dfrac{hb}{e}$

16. $c(a + b)$

17. $m(h + k)$

18. $\dfrac{mu}{y}$

19. $t(h - k)$

20. $(z + t)(a + b)$

21. $\dfrac{e}{t}$

22. $\dfrac{b}{a}$

23. $\dfrac{h}{m}$

24. $\dfrac{bc}{a}$

25. $\dfrac{ud}{c}$

26. $\dfrac{m}{t^2}$

27. $\dfrac{h}{\sin 20°}$

28. $\dfrac{e}{\cos 40°}$

29. $\dfrac{m}{\tan 46°}$

30. $\dfrac{b^2 c^2}{a^2}$

Exercise 17   *page 64*

1. $\pm\sqrt{\dfrac{h}{c}}$

2. $\pm\sqrt{\dfrac{f}{b}}$

3. $\pm\sqrt{\dfrac{m}{t}}$

4. $\pm\sqrt{\dfrac{a + b}{y}}$

5. $\pm\sqrt{\dfrac{t + a}{m}}$

6. $\pm\sqrt{(a + b)}$

7. $\pm\sqrt{(t - c)}$

8. $\pm\sqrt{(z - y)}$

9. $\pm\sqrt{(a^2 + b^2)}$

10. $\pm\sqrt{(m^2 - t^2)}$

11. $\pm\sqrt{(a^2 - n^2)}$

12. $\pm\sqrt{\dfrac{c}{a}}$

13. $\pm\sqrt{\dfrac{n}{h}}$

14. $\pm\sqrt{\dfrac{z + k}{c}}$

15. $\pm\sqrt{\dfrac{c - b}{a}}$

16. $\pm\sqrt{\dfrac{h + e}{d}}$

17. $\pm\sqrt{\dfrac{m + n}{g}}$

18. $\pm\sqrt{\dfrac{z - y}{m}}$

19. $\pm\sqrt{\dfrac{f - a}{m}}$

20. $\pm\sqrt{(b^2 - a^2)}$

21. $a - y$

22. $h - m$

23. $z - q$

24. $b - v$

25. $k - m$

26. $\dfrac{h - d}{c}$

27. $\dfrac{y - c}{m}$

28. $\dfrac{k - h}{e}$

29. $\dfrac{a^2 - d}{b}$

30. $\dfrac{m^2 - n^2}{t}$

31. $\dfrac{v^2 - w}{a}$

32. $y - y^2$

33. $\dfrac{k - m}{t^2}$

34. $\dfrac{b - e}{c}$

35. $\dfrac{h - z}{g}$

36. $\dfrac{c - a - b}{d}$

37. $\dfrac{v^2 - y^2}{k}$

38. $\dfrac{d - h}{f}$

39. $\dfrac{ab - c}{a}$

40. $\dfrac{hm - n}{h}$

Exercise 18   *page 65*

1. $\dfrac{h + d}{a}$

2. $\dfrac{m - k}{z}$

3. $\dfrac{f - ed}{d}$

4. $\dfrac{d - ma}{m}$

5. $\dfrac{c - a}{b}$

6. $\pm\sqrt{\left(\dfrac{b}{a}\right)}$

7. $\pm\sqrt{\left(\dfrac{z}{y}\right)}$

8. $\pm\sqrt{(e + c)}$

9. $\dfrac{b + n}{m}$

10. $\dfrac{b - a^2}{a}$

11. $\dfrac{a}{d}$

12. mt

13. mn

14. $\dfrac{y}{d}$

15. $\dfrac{a}{t}$

16. $\dfrac{d}{n}$

17. $k(a + b)$

18. $\dfrac{v}{y}$

19. $\dfrac{m}{c}$

20. $\pm\sqrt{mb}$

21. $\dfrac{b - ag}{g}$

22. $\dfrac{x^2 - h^2}{h}$

23. $y - z$

24. $\pm\sqrt{\left(\dfrac{c}{m}\right)}$

25. $\dfrac{t - ay}{a}$ **26.** $\dfrac{y^2 + t^2}{u}$ **27.** $\pm \sqrt{(c - t)}$ **28.** $k - m$ **29.** $\dfrac{b - c}{a}$

30. $\dfrac{c - am}{m}$ **31.** $pq - ab$ **32.** $\dfrac{a^2 - t}{b}$ **33.** $\dfrac{w}{v^2}$ **34.** $t - c$

35. $\dfrac{t}{x}$ **36.** $\dfrac{k - mn}{m}$ **37.** $\dfrac{v - t}{x}$ **38.** $\dfrac{c - ab}{a}$ **39.** $\dfrac{ma - e}{m}$

40. $\pm \sqrt{\dfrac{c}{b}}$ **41.** $\dfrac{a}{q}$ **42.** $\pm \sqrt{\left(\dfrac{a}{e}\right)}$ **43.** $\pm \sqrt{\left(\dfrac{h}{m}\right)}$ **44.** $\pm \sqrt{\left(\dfrac{v}{n}\right)}$

45. $\dfrac{v - t^3}{a}$ **46.** $\dfrac{b^3 - a^3}{a}$ **47.** $\pm \sqrt{\left(\dfrac{b + d}{a}\right)}$ **48.** $\dfrac{bc - h^2}{h}$ **49.** $\pm \sqrt{(u^2 - v^2)}$

50. $\dfrac{mb - b^3}{m}$

Exercise 19   page 65

1. $p - a$ **2.** $m - y$ **3.** $z - k$ **4.** $u^2 - t^2$

5. $\dfrac{a - bc}{m}$ **6.** $\dfrac{z - k}{a}$ **7.** $\dfrac{u^2 - e^2}{k}$ **8.** $\dfrac{b - ma}{m}$

9. $\dfrac{h - ka}{k}$ **10.** $\dfrac{y - p^2}{p}$ **11.** ky **12.** mn

13. q^2 **14.** mn^2 **15.** $\dfrac{m}{a}$ **16.** $\dfrac{n}{e}$

17. $\dfrac{u}{w}$ **18.** $\dfrac{e}{\sin 32°}$ **19.** $\dfrac{2y}{z}$ **20.** $\dfrac{3p}{k}$

21. $\pm \sqrt{(m + n)}$ **22.** $\pm \sqrt{(a - b - v)}$ **23.** $\pm \sqrt{\left(\dfrac{n^2 + n}{b}\right)}$ **24.** $\dfrac{d + e + ab}{a}$

25. $\pm \sqrt{\left(\dfrac{mp + k^2}{k}\right)}$ **26.** $y - m$ **27.** $\dfrac{u + ed}{e}$ **28.** $\dfrac{z - ay}{a}$

29. $\dfrac{w + yf}{ye}$ **30.** $\dfrac{m - tm}{at}$ **31.** $y(c + d)$ **32.** $\dfrac{a - b}{p}$

33. $\dfrac{m + n}{A}$ **34.** $\pm \sqrt{\dfrac{k}{h}}$ **35.** $\dfrac{A + B}{E}$ **36.** $\dfrac{4q}{k}$

37. $\pm \sqrt{\left(\dfrac{h + ad}{a}\right)}$ **38.** $k^2 - y$ **39.** $\dfrac{m - g}{n}$ **40.** $\dfrac{c^2 - k}{c}$

Exercise 20   page 66

1. $2(3x + 2y)$ **2.** $3(3x + 4y)$ **3.** $2(5a + 2b)$ **4.** $4(x + 3y)$
5. $5(2a + 3b)$ **6.** $6(3x - 4y)$ **7.** $4(2u - 7v)$ **8.** $5(3s + 5t)$
9. $8(3m - 5n)$ **10.** $9(3c - 8d)$ **11.** $4(5a + 2b)$ **12.** $6(5x - 4y)$
13. $3(9c - 11d)$ **14.** $7(5u + 7v)$ **15.** $4(3s - 8t)$ **16.** $8(5x - 2t)$
17. $12(2x + 7y)$ **18.** $4(3x + 2y + 4z)$ **19.** $3(4a - 2b + 3c)$ **20.** $5(2x - 4y + 5z)$
21. $4(5a - 3b - 7c)$ **22.** $8(6m + n - 3x)$ **23.** $7(6x + 7y - 3z)$ **24.** $3(2x^2 + 5y^2)$
25. $5(4x^2 - 3y^2)$ **26.** $7(a^2 + 4b^2)$ **27.** $9(3a + 7b - 4c)$
28. $6(2x^2 + 4xy + 3y^2)$ **29.** $8(8p - 9q - 5r)$ **30.** $12(3x - 5y + 8z)$

Exercise 21   page 66

1. $x(3x + 2)$
2. $x(4x - 3)$
3. $x(5x + 1)$
4. $x(x - 2)$
5. $y(2y + 5)$
6. $a(4a - 5)$
7. $2x(3x - 1)$
8. $3x(4x + 3)$
9. $2y(5y - 3)$
10. $x(7x - 3)$
11. $5y(2y - 11)$
12. $3a(4a + 7)$
13. $x(x^2 + 2x + 5)$
14. $2x(x^2 - 3x + 1)$
15. $3x(x^2 + x + 2)$
16. $2y(y^2 - 5)$
17. $4t(3t^2 - 7)$
18. $u(u^2 + 2u + 7)$
19. $4x(x^2 - 2x - 1)$
20. $a(3x + 2y)$
21. $x(4a + 3b)$
22. $y(5c + 2d)$
23. $m(4x - 3y)$
24. $n(a + 3b)$
25. $2x(a - 5b)$
26. $3a(2x + y)$
27. $4c(3a + 4b)$
28. $3m(2x + y + z)$
29. $4p(3x - y + 3z)$
30. $5x(2x^2 - x + 2)$
31. $2m(3a^2 + 2a + 1)$
32. $3y(2x^2 + 3x + 4)$
33. $w(4x - 5y - 2z)$
34. $2t(4a - 6b + 7c)$
35. $8y(2x + y + 3)$
36. $5x(3a + 4b - 5)$
37. $9x(4x^2 - 3)$
38. $15x(3a - 2b + 4c)$
39. $12y(7x^2 + 2)$
40. $9u(2x^2 + 3y^2 + 5z^2)$

Exercise 22   page 66

1. 49
2. 9
3. 1
4. 100
5. 10 000
6. 81
7. 400
8. 0.01
9. 0.04
10. 64
11. 25
12. 16
13. 3600
14. 144
15. $\frac{1}{4}$
16. 2
17. 3
18. 10
19. 30
20. 11
21. 6
22. 100
23. 1000
24. 12
25. 1
26. 7
27. 0.1
28. 13
29. $\frac{1}{3}$
30. 0
31. 1
32. 9
33. 25
34. 18
35. 32
36. 10 010
37. 67
38. 30
39. 0
40. 5
41. 40
42. 5
43. 13
44. 10
45. 3

Exercise 23   page 67

1. 1.41
2. 2.24
3. 4.12
4. 2.45
5. 3.16
6. 10.0
7. 2.39
8. 2.87
9. 14.1
10. 20.7
11. 4.31
12. 0.970
13. 0.458
14. 3.46
15. 77.9
16. 230
17. 20.7
18. 0.276
19. 0.308
20. 0.0860
21. 0.0918
22. 1.05
23. 4
24. 1.54
25. 89.8
26. 160
27. 248
28. 1580
29. 0.917
30. 268
31. 16.3
32. 1.33
33. 1.73
34. 4.43
35. 3.35
36. 0.272
37. 2.94
38. 247
39. 48.3
40. 200
41. 6
42. 0.1
43. 2.80
44. 0.0922
45. 922
46. 88.2
47. 482
48. 31.7
49. 0.394
50. 9.37
51. 44.7
52. 218
53. 2.65
54. 41.4
55. (a) 0.141   (b) 0.447   (c) 1.41   (d) 4.47   (e) 14.1   (f) 44.7
56. (a) 0.224   (b) 0.707   (c) 2.24   (d) 7.07   (e) 22.4   (f) 70.7
57. (a) 0.130   (b) 0.412   (c) 1.30   (d) 4.12   (e) 13.0   (f) 41.2
58. (a) 0.0245   (b) 0.0775   (c) 0.245   (d) 0.775   (e) 2.45   (f) 7.75

Exercise 24   page 67

1. 2.08
2. 2.22
3. 3.14
4. 3.91
5. 2.47
6. 4.64
7. 1.26
8. 6.69
9. 0.464
10. 0.215
11. 34.2
12. 92.8

Exercise 25   page 67

1. 3^4
2. 5^2
3. 6^3
4. 10^5
5. 1^7
6. 8^4
7. 7^6
8. $2^3 \times 5^2$
9. $3^2 \times 7^4$
10. $3^2 \times 10^3$
11. $5^4 \times 11^2$
12. $2^2 \times 3^3$
13. $3^2 \times 5^3$
14. $2^2 \times 3^3 \times 11^2$
15. $2^3 \times 3^2 \times 7^2$
16. $2^3 \times 5^3 \times 7$
17. $3^4 \times 5 \times 11^2$
18. $5^2 \times 6^3$
19. $2^3 \times 3^2 \times 7^2$
20. $2 \times 5^2 \times 7^2 \times 9^2$
21. a^3
22. c^4
23. e^5
24. $y^2 \times z^3$
25. $m^3 \times n^2$
26. $t^4 \times p^2$
27. $u^3 \times y^2$
28. $m^2 \times y^4$
29. $a^2 \times e^3 \times y$
30. $e^4 \times n^3$

Exercise 26   *page 68*

1. 8	**2.** 9	**3.** 1	**4.** 27	**5.** 25
6. 4	**7.** 1	**8.** 100	**9.** 16	**10.** 64
11. 1000	**12.** 32	**13.** 81	**14.** 125	**15.** 1 000 000
16. 49	**17.** 4	**18.** 1	**19.** −1	**20.** −8
21. −27	**22.** −1	**23.** 25	**24.** −1000	**25.** −64
26. 64	**27.** 1	**28.** 10 000	**29.** 0.01	**30.** $\frac{1}{4}$

Exercise 27   *page 68*

1. $\frac{1}{4}$	**2.** $\frac{1}{16}$	**3.** $\frac{1}{100}$	**4.** 1	**5.** $\frac{1}{27}$	**6.** $\frac{1}{64}$	**7.** $\frac{1}{1000}$	**8.** $\frac{1}{25}$
9. $\frac{1}{49}$	**10.** $\frac{1}{125}$	**11.** $\frac{1}{81}$	**12.** 1	**13.** T	**14.** F	**15.** T	**16.** T
17. F	**18.** F	**19.** F	**20.** T	**21.** T	**22.** T	**23.** F	**24.** F
25. F	**26.** T	**27.** T	**28.** T	**29.** T	**30.** T	**31.** T	**32.** F
33. T	**34.** T	**35.** F	**36.** T	**37.** F	**38.** F	**39.** T	**40.** F
41. F	**42.** T						

Exercise 28   *page 68*

1. 5^6	**2.** 6^5	**3.** 10^9	**4.** 7^8	**5.** 3^{10}	**6.** 8^6	**7.** 2^{13}
8. 3^4	**9.** 5^3	**10.** 7^4	**11.** 5^2	**12.** 3^{-4}	**13.** 6^5	**14.** 5^{-10}
15. 7^6	**16.** 7^2	**17.** 6^5	**18.** 8^1	**19.** 5^8	**20.** 10^2	**21.** 9^{-2}
22. 3^{-2}	**23.** 2^2	**24.** 3^{-2}	**25.** 7^{-6}	**26.** 3^{-4}	**27.** 5^{-5}	**28.** 8^{-5}
29. 5^{-5}	**30.** 6^2	**31.** 7^8	**32.** 6^4	**33.** 11^{-2}	**34.** 5^{-5}	**35.** 3^5
36. 7^7	**37.** 3^6	**38.** 10^4	**39.** 5^{22}	**40.** 2^5	**41.** 3^6	**42.** 5
43. 7^2	**44.** 5^{-7}	**45.** 2^6				

PART 5

Exercise 1   *page 70*

1. 98 miles	**2.** 2 h	**3.** 40 m.p.h.	**4.** 49 miles	**5.** 9 h
6. 30 m.p.h.	**7.** 62 miles	**8.** 11 h	**9.** 2.65 m.p.h.	**10.** 35.2 miles
11. $4\frac{1}{2}$ h	**12.** 12 m.p.h.	**13.** $62\frac{1}{2}$ miles	**14.** $1\frac{1}{2}$ h	**15.** $13\frac{1}{4}$ m.p.h.

Exercise 2   *page 71*

1. 2 s	**2.** 4 km/h	**3.** 5 h	**4.** 1500 cm	**5.** 7.5 km/h
6. 20 m	**7.** 45.6 km	**8.** 36 km/h	**9.** 180 feet	**10.** 0.06 cm/s
11. 6 h	**12.** 4 m	**13.** 10 days	**14.** 0.5 m	**15.** 400 km/h
16. 2 km	**17.** 40 km/h	**18.** 0.01 s	**19.** 0.5 s	**20.** 75 m
21. 30 s	**22.** 6 s	**23.** 0.02 m/s	**24.** 62.5 miles	**25.** 54 m.p.h.

Exercise 3   *page 71*

1. 30 miles	**2.** 36 km	**3.** 120 km	**4.** 32 miles
5. 3 miles	**6.** 400 miles	**7.** 50 miles	**8.** 10 km

9. (a) $\frac{1}{2}$ h   (b) $\frac{1}{4}$ h   (c) $\frac{3}{4}$ h   (d) 5 s
10. (a) 124 miles   (b) 68 km   (c) 42 miles   (d) 30 km
11. (a) 34 km/h   (b) 88 km/h   (c) 45 km/h   (d) 69 km/h
12. (a) $9\frac{1}{2}$ miles   (b) $9\frac{1}{2}$ miles   (c) 12 km   (d) 16 km
13. 5.1 h   **14.** 3 h 20 mins   **15.** (a) 12 25   (b) 225 km   **16.** 385 m
17. (a) 80 km/h   (b) 135 km   (c) 90 km/h   (d) 2000

Exercise 4   *page 72*

1. 5 cm	**2.** 7.81 cm	**3.** 10.6 cm	**4.** 5.66 cm	**5.** 8.60 cm	**6.** 8.06 cm
7. 12.0 cm	**8.** 7.62 cm	**9.** 13 cm	**10.** 8.49 cm	**11.** 4.58 cm	**12.** 5.20 cm
13. 6.24 cm	**14.** 4.47 cm	**15.** 12 cm	**16.** 6 cm	**17.** 8.49 cm	**18.** 3.77 cm
19. 12 cm	**20.** 6.11 cm				

Exercise 5   *page 73*

1. 6.63 cm	**2.** 10.4 cm	**3.** 5.57 cm	**4.** 10.9 cm	**5.** 8.54 cm	**6.** 17.2 cm
7. 8.54 cm	**8.** 9.54 cm				

Exercise 6   *page 74*

1. 19.2 km	**2.** 427 km	**3.** 4.58 m	**4.** 9.75 km	**5.** 5.20 m	**6.** 9.43 cm
7. 6.63 cm	**8.** 7.60 cm	**9.** 36.1 m	**10.** (a) 5 cm	(b) 7.81 cm	
11. (a) 8.06 cm	(b) 9 cm	**12.** (b) 11.4 cm			

Exercise 7   *page 74*

1. (a) (i) $2.50   (ii) $2   (iii) $3
    (b) (i) £0.80   (ii) £2.80   (iii) £2
2. (a) (i) DM4   (ii) DM12   (iii) DM6
    (b) (i) £2   (ii) £2.50   (iii) £0.50   (c) DM10
3. (a) (i) 2.5 kg   (ii) 3.6 kg   (iii) 0.9 kg
    (b) (i) 4.4 lb   (ii) 6.6 lb   (iii) 3.3 lb   (c) 2.2 lb
    (d) 4.1 kg
4. (a) (i) 9.1 l   (ii) 6.3 l   (iii) 12.7 l
    (b) (i) 2.2 gallons   (ii) 1.5 gallons   (iii) 0.9 gallons   (c) 13.6
    (d) car B (11 l to 10.9 l)
5. (a) (i) 1.6 km   (ii) 4.8 km   (iii) 3.5 km
    (b) (i) 1.25 miles   (ii) 3.1 miles   (iii) 2.2 miles
    (c) John (2 miles = 3.2 km)   (d) Jane (2.7 miles = 4.3 km)

Exercise 8   *page 76*

1. $\frac{1}{5}, \frac{5}{2}, -\frac{4}{3}$ **2.** $\frac{4}{5}, -\frac{1}{6}, -5$
3. AB : 4; BC : $\frac{1}{2}$; AC : $-\frac{2}{3}$; DE : $\frac{2}{3}$; EF : -5; DF : $-\frac{3}{4}$; GH : 1; HI : $-\frac{1}{4}$; GI : -4; JK : 0; JL : $-\frac{4}{3}$; KL : 4.
4. (a) 5   (b) $\frac{2}{3}$ (c) $-\frac{3}{7}$ (d) $-\frac{8}{5}$ (e) -1
    (f) $\frac{3}{11}$ (g) 0   (h) -10 (i) 0   (j) -4
    (k) infinite   (l) infinite   **5.** (b) -2.5 (c) -0.625 **6.** (b) 2   (c) 6

Exercise 10   *page 79*

1. (c) (i) $x = 4$ (ii) $x = 3$ (iii) $x = -2$ (iv) $x = 1.5$ (v) $x = 2$ (vi) $x = 3$
2. (c) (i) 7   (ii) 0   (iii) 4   (iv) 5   (v) 3.5   (vi) 2.5
    (vii) 3   (viii) 4
3. (c) (i) 7   (ii) 2   (iii) 2.5   (iv) 4   (v) 1   (vi) 8
    (vii) 5
4. (c) (i) 2.3, -4.3 (ii) $-5, 3$ (iii) no solutions   (iv) $-4.4, 3.4$
5. (c) (i) ±3.16 (ii) ±2.45 (iii) ±1.73 (iv) $-2, 3$ (v) $-3.7, 2.7$
6. (c) (i) 1.3   (ii) ±2.8 (iii) ±2 (iv) 1.2, 6.8
7. (c) (i) -1.14 (ii) $-1.24, 3.24$ (iii) ±2.83
8. (c) (i) $-1.8, 2.8$ (ii) $-2.7, 3.7$ (iii) $-1, 3$ (iv) $-3.2, 2.2$

Exercise 11   *page 80*

1. $x = 2, y = 4$ **2.** $x = 2, y = 3$ **3.** $x = 5, y = 3$ **4.** $x = 3, y = 2$
5. $x = 4, y = 3$ **6.** $x = 3, y = 1$ **7.** $x = 1, y = 5$

PART 6

Exercise 1   *page 83*

1. (a) 90° clockwise, (0, 0)   (b) 90° anticlockwise, (1, 1)
   (c) 180°, (0, 0)   (d) 90° clockwise, (−2, 1)
2. (a) 90° clockwise, (0, 0)   (b) 180° (2, 4)
   (c) 90° clockwise, (3, 2)   (d) 180°, (2, −1)
   (e) 90° clockwise, (−1, 0)   (f) 90° anticlockwise, (4, 5)
   (g) 90° anticlockwise, (0, 0)
3. (a) 90° clockwise, (2, 2)   (b) 180°, (−2, −1)
   (c) 90° clockwise, (−3, −3)   (d) 90° anticlockwise, (−1, −1)
   (e) 90° anticlockwise, (−2, −2)   (f) 90° anticlockwise, (0, −2)
   (g) 180°, (−1, 2)   (h) 90° anticlockwise, (−3, −3)
4. (a) *x*-axis   (b) $x = -1$ (c) $y = x$ (d) *y*-axis   (e) $y = -1$ (f) $y = x$
5. (a) rotation 90° clockwise, (0, 2)   (b) translation $\begin{pmatrix} 10 \\ -3 \end{pmatrix}$

   (c) reflection in $y = x$ (d) reflection in *x* axis
   (e) rotation 90° anticlockwise, $(6\frac{1}{2}, 5\frac{1}{2})$ (f) rotation 90° clockwise, (0, 0)
6. (a) reflection in $y = 1$ (b) reflection in $y = -x$

   (c) rotation 90° clockwise, (0, 0)   (d) translation $\begin{pmatrix} -4 \\ 10 \end{pmatrix}$

   (e) rotation 90° anticlockwise, (−7, 3)   (f) reflection in $y = x$
   (g) rotation 180°, (0, 1)   (h) reflection in *y* axis

7. (a) rotation 90° clockwise, (4, −2)   (b) translation $\begin{pmatrix} 8 \\ 2 \end{pmatrix}$

   (c) reflection in $y = x$ (d) enlargement; scale factor $\frac{1}{2}$, (7, −7)
   (e) rotation 90° anticlockwise, (−8, 0)   (f) enlargement; scale factor 2, (−1, −9)
   (g) rotation 90° anticlockwise, (7, 3)

   Congruent to △1 : △2, △3, △4, △6

8. (a) enlargement; scale factor $1\frac{1}{2}$, (1, −4)   (b) rotation 90° clockwise, (0, −4)

   (c) reflection in $y = -x$ (d) translation $\begin{pmatrix} 11 \\ 10 \end{pmatrix}$

   (e) enlargement; scale factor $\frac{1}{2}$, (−3, 8)   (f) rotation 90° anticlockwise, $(\frac{1}{2}, 6\frac{1}{2})$
   (g) enlargement; scale factor 3, (−2, 5)

   Congruent to △1 : △3, △4, △5.

Exercise 2   *page 84*

1. (c) (i) (−1, 2)   (ii) (−2, −1)   (iii) (2, −4)   (iv) (4, −2)
2. (c) (ii) (8, 5)   (ii) (8, −5)   (iii) (−8, 2)   (iv) (−3, 0)
3. (c) (i) (6, 8)   (ii) (6, −2)   (iii) (−2, −8)   (iv) (−2, −2)
4. (c) (ii) (6, 0)   (ii) (2, −8)   (iii) (−8, 2)   (iv) (1, −5)   (v) (−1, 3)
5. (c) (ii) (5, 8)   (ii) (−1, 8)   (iii) (−4, 1)   (iv) (−8, −5)   (v) (4, −7)

Test 1   *page 86*

1. £3.50   2. £4.95   3. 48   4. 10p, 10p, 20p   5. $6\frac{1}{2}$
6. $\frac{1}{100}$ 7. 56   8. 75%   9. 15   10. 56p
11. 50 min   12. 6.5   13. 130 m   14. 770   15. 11
16. 25   17. $1\frac{1}{4}$ 18. £10   19. 10   20. 60.5

21. Decimal **22.** 16 **23.** 1 h **24.** $4\frac{1}{2}$ **25.** 75 or 105
26. 20 **27.** £2.40 **28.** 841 **29.** £4000 **30.** 48p

Test 2   *page 86*

1. 96 **2.** 19 **3.** 06 30 **4.** £2.75 **5.** £1.90
6. 30 **7.** 5 018 001 **8.** 15 **9.** £6 **10.** 3.5p
11. 53 **12.** 800 g **13.** 74 **14.** 280 miles **15.** 40
16. 4 **17.** 62 **18.** 5 **19.** 5 **20.** 480
21. 158 **22.** 95 **23.** 0.2 **24.** 0.7 **25.** £84
26. £2455 **27.** 64 **28.** 90p **29.** 55 m.p.h. **30.** 28

Test 3   *page 87*

1. 70 **2.** 240 **3.** 900 **4.** 10 705 **5.** 10 45 **6.** 245
7. 20 **8.** £3.05 **9.** £1.76 **10.** 20, 20, 20, 1 or 50, 5, 5, 1
11. 0.75 **12.** 5 **13.** Tuesday **14.** 1.5 kg **15.** £150.50 **16.** 640 m
17. £722 **18.** £25 000 **19.** 4 **20.** £1.10 **21.** 28 **22.** 9
23. 91 **24.** £6 **25.** 98p **26.** £4.46 **27.** £3.30 **28.** £42
29. 960 **30.** 18p

Test 4   *page 88*

1. £8.05 **2.** 75 **3.** 25 **4.** 0.1 cm **5.** 24p **6.** 104
7. 40p **8.** £88 **9.** 5:50 **10.** £8.20 **11.** 4 km **12.** 45 miles
13. £4.25 **14.** 998 **15.** 20 **16.** 200 **17.** 22.5 cm **18.** 75p
19. 10 **20.** 16 **21.** 20 **22.** £9.82 **23.** 22 min **24.** 1540
25. £7.94 **26.** 70p **27.** 200 **28.** 35% **29.** 100 **30.** £2500

Test 5   *page 88*

1. 360 **2.** £9.05 **3.** 12 **4.** 1.5p **5.** 9:35 **6.** 29
7. 140 **8.** 57 **9.** 82 **10.** 30p **11.** Diagonal **12.** 95°
13. 24 **14.** £9 **15.** 7:35 **16.** 244 **17.** £4.16 **18.** 90
19. 55 **20.** 45 miles **21.** 24 cm **22.** 185 cm **23.** $1\frac{1}{2}$ **24.** £200
25. −2°C **26.** 16 **27.** £6850 **28.** £7.80 **29.** 499 mm **30.** 8 027 010

Test 6   *page 89*

1. 1050 **2.** 3:38 **3.** £9.35 **4.** 29 **5.** £6.50 **6.** 21
7. 400 **8.** −8°C **9.** 210 **10.** £10 **11.** 153 **12.** £2000
13. 12 **14.** 45 **15.** 20p **16.** 240 **17.** Equation
18. 50, 10, 1, 1 or 20, 20, 20, 2 or 50, 5, 5, 2 **19.** £3.55 **20.** 1916 **21.** 4:30
22. £2.75 **23.** 900 g **24.** 155 **25.** 49° **26.** 104 **27.** £670
28. 06 15 **29.** 150 miles **30.** 20

Test 7   *page 90*

1. 27 **2.** £12.50 **3.** 16 **4.** 170 **5.** 3 017 004
6. 120 **7.** 19 22 **8.** 250 **9.** 0.03 **10.** £245
11. £7.90 **12.** 4.5p **13.** $\frac{1}{2}$ gallon **14.** 210 **15.** 20%
16. £8.14 **17.** 93 **18.** 40p **19.** 5 **20.** 11
21. 175 cm **22.** 150 **23.** 61 **24.** 38 **25.** £13.50
26. £4.50 **27.** 80 m.p.h. **28.** £12 → £13 **29.** 1908 **30.** 2997 m

Test 8   *page 90*

1. 9 **2.** £3.80 **3.** 50 **4.** 50 **5.** 72 **6.** 90°
7. 148 **8.** $8\frac{1}{2}$ **9.** 4000 **10.** $\frac{1}{1000}$ **11.** 50 **12.** 108

13. $\frac{7}{10}$ **14.** £1.15 **15.** 7 **16.** 20 **17.** 15 024 **18.** 24
19. 7 or 37 **20.** 20 cm **21.** 18 **22.** £4.50 **23.** £9.00 **24.** £4.50
25. £168 **26.** 6 **27.** £18 **28.** 14 **29.** $1\frac{3}{4}$ h **30.** 80%

Test 9   *page 91*

1. 72p **2.** 112 **3.** £6 **4.** 6 **5.** 38 **6.** Friday
7. £11 **8.** 8:45 **9.** 50, 10; 10, 2 or 50, 20, 1, 1 **10.** 0.25 **11.** 9.5
12. 100 **13.** 396 cm **14.** 500 **15.** Parallel **16.** 30 010 **17.** 12
18. £55 500 **19.** 400 **20.** 8 **21.** Circumference **22.** 12 m **23.** 95
24. £6.26 **25.** £2.40 **26.** 90p **27.** 162 **28.** £16 **29.** 300
30. 0.3

Test 10   *page 91*

1. £15.65 **2.** 75 **3.** 100 **4.** 0.01 cm **5.** 12p **6.** 156
7. 60p **8.** £65 **9.** 6:45 **10.** £8.50 **11.** 3 km **12.** 100 miles
13. £3.20 **14.** 999 **15.** 15 miles **16.** 155 **17.** $42\frac{1}{2}$ cm **18.** 60p
19. 5 **20.** 25 **21.** 30 **22.** £9.77 **23.** 26 mins **24.** 15 40
25. £7.55 **26.** 50p **27.** 2500 **28.** 45% **29.** 125 mins **30.** £425

Exercise 3   *page 92*

1. (a) 1 (b) 1 **2.** (a) 1 (b) 1 **3.** (a) 4 (b) 4 **4.** (a) 2 (b) 2
5. (a) 0 (b) 6 **6.** (a) 0 (b) 4 **7.** (a) 0 (b) 2 **8.** (a) 1 (b) 1
9. (a) 4 (b) 4 **10.** (a) 4 (b) 4 **11.** (a) 0 (b) 4 **12.** (a) 0 (b) 2
13. (a) 4 (b) 4 **14.** (a) 4 (b) 4 **15.** (a) 0 (b) 4 **16.** (a) 4 (b) 4
17. (a) 8 (b) 8 **18.** (a) 1 (b) 1 **19.** (a) 5 (b) 5 **20.** (a) 0 (b) 2
21. (a) 0 (b) 2 **22.** (a) 0 (b) 4 **23.** (a) 12 (b) 6 **24.** (a) infinite (b) infinite

Exercise 4   *page 94*

1. 7, 9, 11, 13, 15, 17. 19 **2.** 4, 10, 16, 22, 28, 34, 40
3. 2, 3, 4, 5, 6, 7, 8 **4.** 38, 46, 54, 62, 34, 38, 42
5. 56, 64, 72, 80, 88, 44, 48 **6.** 54, 62, 71, 38, 42, 46, 50
7. 6, 24, 12, 42, 18, 60, 24, 78, 30 **8.** 24, 12, 42, 18, 60, 24, 78, 30, 96

Exercise 5   *page 95*

1. (a) 11, 22, 11, 33 (b) 12, 24, 13, 39 (c) 7, 14, 28, 17, 51
(d) 9, 16, 32, 21, 63 (e) 11, 18, 36, 25, 75 (f) 13, 20, 40, 29, 87
2. (a) 6, 12, 27, 20, 5 (b) 3, 6, 21, 14, $3\frac{1}{2}$ (c) 8, 16, 31, 24, 6
(d) 10, 20, 35, 28, 7 (e) 1, 2, 17, 10, $2\frac{1}{2}$ (f) 12, 24, 39, 32, 8
3. (a) 7, 22, 44, 22, $5\frac{1}{2}$ (b) 10, 25, 50, 28, 7 (c) 16, 31, 62, 40, 10
(d) $\frac{1}{2}$, $15\frac{1}{2}$, 31, 9, $2\frac{1}{4}$ (e) 100, 115, 230, 208, 52 (f) 24, 39, 78, 56, 14
4. (a) 4, 16, 48, 38, 19 (b) 5, 25, 75, 65, $32\frac{1}{2}$ (c) 6, 36, 108, 98, 49
(d) 8, 64, 192, 182, 91 (e) 1, 1, 3, -7, $-3\frac{1}{2}$ (f) 10, 100, 300, 290, 145

THINK ABOUT IT   2

Project 1   *page 97*

(a) cut out 4 cm squares   (b) 3.5 cm, $3\frac{1}{3}$ cm. Always $\frac{1}{6} \times$ side of square card.   (c) 2.43 cm (3 s.f.)

Exercise A   *page 98*

1. 600 **2.** £2.60 **3.** (a) 720 000 (b) 200 **4.** 50 m

5. 5 h 34 min   **6.** (a) $6^2 = 5^2 + 11, 7^2 = 6^2 + 13$ (b) $11^2 = 60 + 5^2 + 6^2, 13^2 = 84 + 6^2 + 7^2$
7. $\frac{2}{3}$ is larger   **8.** (a) 132 cm   (b) 140 cm   **9.** (a) 120   (b) 480
10. (a) 320   (b) £592

Exercise B   *page 100*

1. (a) 72 kg   (b) 18 kg   **2.** £3.40   **3.** (a) 22   (b) £187   (c) 50
4. (a) £100   (b) 142.5 kg   (c) 48 cm   **5.** (a) $\frac{1}{10}$ (b) $\frac{1}{4}$ (c) $\frac{1}{100}$ **6.** 80°
7. (a) £1.89   (b) £14.49   **8.** (a) 80 g   (b) 5.2   (c) 416
9. (a) 1875 km   (b) 2 h 12 min   **10.** (a) 450   (b) £9750

Project 3   *page 101*

Part A

7	7	7	■	2	9	■	1
5	■	3	9	8	1	■	5
6	0	5	■	0	■	7	8
1	■	8	5	8	■	0	■
■	6	0	8	■	4	0	7
6	7	■	8	6	8	■	■
1	■	1	■	1	7	4	6
5	7	2	■	5	■	4	9

Part B

8	4	2	■	7	4	■	3
1	■	4	8	8	4	■	1
3	3	6	■	3	■	5	7
7	■	1	2	0	■	2	■
■	5	0	9	■	7	2	4
5	8	■	7	2	0	■	■
9	■	1	■	6	8	6	4
2	5	7	■	5	■	4	7

Part C

1	6	1	■	3	6	■	3
7	■	6	4	5	8	■	4
8	6	4	■	0	■	2	8
5	■	3	6	0	■	6	■
■	6	3	7	■	8	0	5
2	5	■	1	2	4	■	■
5	■	3	■	3	1	1	1
9	9	9	■	4	■	6	3

Part D

5	9	2	■	3	7	■	4
5	■	5	1	9	4	■	2
3	7	6	■	5	■	9	9
2	■	8	2	6	■	2	■
■	2	4	0	■	1	4	5
3	9	■	5	6	3	■	■
2	■	1	■	8	4	7	5
4	6	2	■	5	■	4	7

Exercise C   *page 103*

1. 4.3   **2.** 0.7   **3.** 9.4   **4.** 7   **5.** 42   **6.** 1.2   **7.** 3.3
8. 16   **9.** 23.4   **10.** 17.4   **11.** 128   **12.** 54   **13.** 8   **14.** 2.6
15. 24   **16.** 120   **17.** 1.8   **18.** 190   **19.** 15.2   **20.** 0.2   **21.** 5.5
22. 0.5   **23.** 1.2   **24.** 1.75   **25.** 6.5   **26.** 10.75   **27.** 15   **28.** 11
29. 8.6   **30.** 0.24   **31.** 53   **32.** 1.76   **33.** 3.13   **34.** 47.5   **35.** 4.35
36. 22   **37.** 1.92   **38.** 92   **39.** 76   **40.** 105   **41.** 50   **42.** 1.9
43. 2.5   **44.** 1200   **45.** 1.6   **46.** 3.75   **47.** 7.625   **48.** 5.2   **49.** 1330
50. 08 40   **51.** 14 10   **52.** 04 50   **53.** 12 20   **54.** 18 20   **55.** 11 00   **56.** 08 20
57. 11 20   **58.** 13 00

Project 4   *page 105*

1. Sell	**2.** Slosh	**3.** Bell	**4.** Goes	**5.** Hole
6. Hello	**7.** Geese	**8.** Legible	**9.** Obsess	**10.** Oboe
11. She lies	**12.** Big log	**13.** Loose	**14.** Biggish	**15.** Eggshell
16. Igloo	**17.** Gloss	**18.** Bilge	**19.** Legless	**20.** Shoes
21. Siege	**22.** He did	**23.** Oblige	**24.** Libel	**25.** Besiege
26. He is so big	**27.** Boo Hoo	**28.** Booze	**29.** Eel	**30.** Goose
31. Goodbie	**32.** He sells			

Exercise D   *page 106*

1. (a) 170   (b) £44.20   **2.** 120 g   **3.** $1\frac{3}{20}$ **4.** 84 cm^2
5. (a) £4.40   (b) £10.56   **6.** shirt £9, tie £2   **7.** (a) $\frac{2}{15}$ (b) $\frac{7}{8}$ (c) $\frac{1}{9}$
8. (a) $8 - 2 \times (3 - 1)$
   (b) $(8 - 2) \times (3 - 1)$ (c) $8 - (2 \times 3 - 1)$
9. (a) $(9 + 2) \times 4 - 3$
   (b) $9 + 2 \times (4 - 3)$ or $(9 + 2) \times (4 - 3)$
10. (a) $(12 - 5) \times (2 + 4)$
   (b) $(12 - 5) \times 2 + 4$ (c) $12 - 5 \times (2 + 4)$
   (d) $12 - (5 \times 2 + 4)$

Project 5   *page 107*

1. 2	**2.** 3	**3.** 2	**4.** 2	**5.** 2	**6.** 3	**7.** 6	**8.** 1

Exercise E   *page 108*

1. $\frac{36}{54}$ **2.** $\frac{119}{138}$ **3.** $\frac{95}{115}$ **4.** $\frac{135}{435}$ **5.** $\frac{217}{370}$ **6.** $\frac{189}{356}$
7. (a) $\frac{27}{32}, \frac{17}{20}, \frac{7}{8}$ (b) $\frac{1}{5}, \frac{21}{100}, \frac{9}{40}$ (c) $\frac{3}{4}, \frac{5}{6}, \frac{6}{7}$ (d) $\frac{5}{9}, \frac{2}{3}, \frac{8}{11}$ (e) $\frac{3}{4}, \frac{7}{9}, \frac{13}{15}, \frac{11}{12}$
   (f) $\frac{3}{5}, \frac{17}{23}, \frac{15}{19}$ (g) $\frac{4}{13}, \frac{7}{19}, \frac{5}{11}, \frac{17}{37}$
8. $\frac{7}{9}$ **9.** $\frac{6}{7}$ **10.** $\frac{7}{12}$ **11.** $\frac{8}{17}$ **12.** $\frac{11}{8}$ **13.** $\frac{13}{9}$ **14.** $\frac{12}{11}$ **15.** $\frac{3}{17}$
16. $\frac{7}{19}$

Project 6   *page 109*

1. 41×32 **2.** 431×52 **3.** $631 \times 542 = 342\ 002$ **4.** $742 \times 6531 = 4\ 846\ 002$
5. $8531 \times 7642 = 65\ 193\ 902$

Exercise F   *page 109*

1. (a) £49   (b) £93.50   (c) 100 km   **2.** (a) £250   (b) £250
3. (b) 102.86°   **4.** (a) 15   (b) 6   (c) £1.50   **5.** 85
6. 000, 001, 010, 011, 100, 101, 110, 111

Project 7   *page 111*

Second number + fourth number = 99 999   ∴ Sum of five numbers = first number + 199 998
Third number + fifth number   = 99 999   = first number + 200 000 − 2

PART 7

Exercise 1   *page 112*

1. 6.2   **2.** 3.875   **3.** 7   **4.** 6   **5.** 1.42   **6.** 7.3   **7.** $\frac{1}{8}$
8. 2757   **9.** 6.3   **10.** 58.25   **11.** 70.4, 73.25, no
12. (a) 6   (b) 6.5   **13.** (a) 6   (b) 5.6
14. (a) 1.15   (b) 0.92   **15.** (a) 5   (b) 5.625
16. (a) 5.25   (b) 5.6   **17.** (a) 7   (b) 6.6

18. (a) 1.6 m   (b) 1.634 m   **19.** (a) 51 kg   (b) 50 kg
20. (a) 7.2   (b) 5   (c) 6

Exercise 2   *page 113*

1. (a) 16.4   (b) 19.2   (c) 3.56   **2.** (a) 21.7   (b) 14.4   (c) 3.61
3. (a) 23.2   (b) 26.4   (c) 4.96   **4.** (a) 13.6   (b) 7.0   (c) 2.29
5. 5.42   **6.** (a) 192 kg   (b) 321 kg   (c) 51.3 kg
7. (a) 5.34 m   (b) 11.13 m   (c) 1.647 m

Exercise 3   *page 114*

1. 4   **2.** 8   **3.** 8   **4.** 4   **5.** 11   **6.** 4
7. 7.5   **8.** 3.5   **9.** 1.2   **10.** 0.81   **11.** 3   **12.** $\frac{1}{2}$
13. $\frac{1}{5}$ **14.** 0.5   **15.** 148 cm   **16.** 3   **17.** 3   **18.** 12

Exercise 4   *page 114*

1. 2   **2.** 3   **3.** 6   **4.** 7   **5.** 7   **6.** 5   **7.** 18p
8. 2°C   **9.** 3   **10.** 6

Exercise 5   *page 115*

1. 4.4, 4, 2   **2.** 5, 6, 8   **3.** 3.625, 3.5, 3   **4.** 1.1, 1.2, 1.8
5. 17.6, 18, 18   **6.** 6.1, 5.5, 4   **7.** 0.45, 0.5, 0.5   **8.** 3, 3, 3
9. 0.625, $\frac{1}{2}$, $\frac{1}{4}$ **10.** 0, −1, −1   **11.** 0.78, 0.8, 0.85   **12.** 1, 0, −1
13. 7, 5, 4   **14.** 11, 11, 13   **15.** 111.2, 102, 101   **16.** 5, 5, 1
17. 0.0884, 0.11, 0.111   **18.** 0.3132, 0.32, 0.322   **19.** 1, 0, −2   **20.** 39, 40, 41

Exercise 6   *page 115*

1. 96.25 g   **2.** 51.9p   **3.** 4.82 cm   **4.** 7.1 cm   **5.** 3.65   **6.** 7.82
7. 1.48 m   **8.** 8.9 s

Exercise 7   *page 117*

1. (a) £210   (b) £70   (c) £105   (d) £35
2. (a) £1333.33   (b) £1500   (c) £666.67   (d) £1000   (e) £1200
3. (a) £21 600 000   (b) £8 000 000   (c) £1 000 000   **4.** 230, 66, 114, 142, 70°, 14°
5. (a) 8 min, 34 min, 10 min   (b) 30°   (c) 18°
6. (a) £62 000   (b) £650 000   (c) £3800   (d) £70 000

Exercise 8   *page 118*

1. (a) (i) 45°   (ii) 200°   (iii) 110°   (iv) 5°   **2.** (a) $\frac{3}{10}$, $\frac{4}{10}$, $\frac{1}{5}$, $\frac{1}{10}$
3. $x = 60°$, $y = 210°$ **4.** Barley 60°, Oats 90°, Rye 165°, Wheat 45°
5. (a) 180°   (b) 36°   (c) 90°   (d) 54°   **6.** BBC1 126°, BBC2 18°, ITV 180°, Channel 4 36°
7. (From top to bottom) 120°, 60°, 100°, 40°, 40°
8. (a) 100°, 40°, 60°, 120°, 40°   (b) 80°, 30°, 100°, 50°, 100°   (c) 90°, 42°, 72°, 96°, 60°
     (d) 200°, 35°, 45°, 25°, 55°   (e) 150°, 24°, 60°, 48°, 78°

Exercise 9   *page 120*

1. (a) £120 000   (b) 1986   (c) 1985   (d) £30 000   (e) £700 000
2. (a) £70 000 000   (b) £40 000 000   (c) £20 000 000   (d) £15 000 000   (e) £84 000 000
3. (a) 5   (b) 19   (c) 23   (d) 55   (e) $\frac{6}{23}$
5. (a) £45 000   (b) £30 000   (c) 3 months   (d) April and May   (e) £115 000
6. Frequency: 2, 4, 5, 7, 9, 13, 6, 0, 5, 6, 3

7. (a) A 6, B 6, C 5, D 6, N 3, P 4, R 6, S 5, T 12, V 9, W 9, X 9. All others 0.   (b) (i) 9   (ii) T
8. (c) 12

Exercise 10   *page 122*

1. B   **2.** D   **3.** (a) C   (b) A   (c) D   (d) B
4. (a) (i) 35 cm   (ii) 57.5 cm   (iii) 42.5 cm   (b) (i) 2 kg   (ii) 2.8 kg   (iii) 1.2 kg
(c) 18 cm approximately   (d) 12.5 cm   **5.** (a) (i) 10°C   (ii) 16°C   (iii) 15.5°C
(b) 5 p.m. and 11 p.m.   (c) 1°C at 3 a.m.   (d) (i) 6 a.m. and 3 p.m.   (ii) 10 a.m. and 10 p.m.
(e) 5°C between 4 p.m. and 5 p.m.   **6.** (c) (i) £34.50   (ii) $2\frac{1}{2}$ h
7. (a) (i) £40   (ii) 250 km   (b) (ii) 200 km   (iii) £15
8. (c) 55 km/h   (d) 6.5   (e) £5.34

Exercise 11   *page 126*

1. (a) $\frac{1}{13}$ (b) $\frac{1}{52}$ (c) $\frac{1}{4}$ **2.** (a) $\frac{1}{9}$ (b) $\frac{1}{3}$ (c) $\frac{4}{9}$ (d) $\frac{2}{9}$
3. (a) $\frac{5}{11}$ (b) $\frac{2}{11}$ (c) $\frac{4}{11}$ **4.** (a) $\frac{4}{17}$ (b) $\frac{3}{17}$ (c) $\frac{11}{17}$
5. (a) $\frac{4}{17}$ (b) $\frac{8}{17}$ (c) $\frac{5}{17}$
6. (a) $\frac{2}{9}$ (b) $\frac{2}{9}$ (c) $\frac{1}{9}$ (d) 0   (e) $\frac{5}{9}$
7. (a) $\frac{1}{13}$ (b) $\frac{2}{13}$ (c) $\frac{1}{52}$ (d) $\frac{5}{52}$ **8.** (a) $\frac{1}{10}$ (b) $\frac{3}{10}$ (c) $\frac{3}{10}$
9. (a) $\frac{3}{13}$ (b) $\frac{5}{13}$ (c) $\frac{8}{13}$ **10.** (a) (i) $\frac{5}{13}$ (ii) $\frac{6}{13}$ (b) (i) $\frac{5}{12}$ (ii) $\frac{5}{12}$
11. (a) $\frac{1}{5}$ (b) $\frac{1}{20}$ (c) $\frac{1}{2}$ (d) $\frac{2}{5}$ **12.** $\frac{9}{20}$

Exercise 12   *page 127*

1. (a) $\frac{1}{17}$ (b) $\frac{4}{17}$ (c) $\frac{1}{51}$ (d) $\frac{1}{51}$
2. (a) $\frac{3}{49}$ (b) $\frac{10}{49}$ (c) $\frac{1}{49}$ (d) $\frac{1}{49}$
3. (a) (i) $\frac{5}{11}$ (ii) $\frac{6}{11}$ (iii) $\frac{7}{11}$ (iv) $\frac{9}{11}$ (b) (i) $\frac{6}{11}$ (ii) $\frac{2}{11}$ (iii) $\frac{5}{11}$
4. (a) $\frac{1}{36}$ (b) $\frac{1}{9}$ (c) $\frac{1}{36}$ (d) $\frac{1}{6}$ (e) $\frac{1}{6}$ (f) $\frac{1}{36}$
5. (a) $\frac{1}{8}$ (b) $\frac{3}{8}$ (c) $\frac{3}{8}$ **6.** (a) $\frac{1}{16}$ (b) $\frac{1}{4}$ (c) $\frac{3}{8}$ (d) $\frac{1}{4}$
7. (a) $\frac{1}{6}$ (b) $\frac{1}{2}$ (c) $\frac{1}{2}$ **8.** (a) (i) $\frac{1}{4}$ (ii) $\frac{1}{4}$ (iii) $\frac{1}{4}$ (b) $\frac{1}{4}$ (c) $\frac{6}{27} = \frac{2}{9}$

Exercise 13   *page 129*

1. (a) $\frac{25}{64}$ (b) $\frac{9}{64}$ **2.** (a) $\frac{9}{49}$ (b) $\frac{16}{49}$ (c) $\frac{12}{49}$
3. (a) $\frac{1}{49}$ (b) $\frac{16}{49}$ (c) $\frac{8}{49}$ (d) $\frac{8}{49}$ **4.** (b) (i) $\frac{20}{56} = \frac{5}{14}$ (ii) $\frac{6}{56} = \frac{3}{28}$
5. (a) $\frac{1}{21}$ (b) $\frac{10}{21}$ (c) $\frac{5}{21}$
6. (a) $\frac{2}{11}$ (b) $\frac{1}{55}$ (c) $\frac{2}{11}$ (d) $\frac{4}{55}$
7. (a) $\frac{8}{125}$ (b) $\frac{27}{125}$ (c) $\frac{12}{125}$ **8.** (a) $\frac{1}{64}$ (b) $\frac{27}{64}$ (c) $\frac{27}{64}$
9. (a) $\frac{1}{216}$ (b) $\frac{125}{216}$ **10.** (a) $\frac{1}{8}$ (b) $\frac{1}{8}$ (c) $\frac{3}{8}$
11. (a) $\frac{1}{5}$ (b) $\frac{7}{10}$ (d) (i) $\frac{1}{4}$ (ii) $\frac{3}{10}$ (iii) $\frac{1}{25}$
12. (a) $\frac{4}{9}$ (b) $\frac{5}{9}$ (c) 16   (d) $\frac{16}{81}$ **13.** (a) $\frac{1}{16}$ (b) $\frac{3}{8}$
14. (a) $\frac{1}{27}$ (b) $\frac{2}{9}$ **15.** (a) (i) $\frac{1}{10}$ (ii) $\frac{1}{4}$ (iii) $\frac{1}{40}$ (iv) $\frac{1}{40}$
(b) $\frac{1}{39}$ (c) $\frac{1}{40} \times \frac{1}{39} = \frac{1}{1560}$

PART 8

Exercise 1   *page 131*

1. 48°   **2.** 134°   **3.** 39°   **4.** 65°   **5.** 31°   **6.** 44°   **7.** 36°
8. 51°   **9.** 100°   **10.** 80°   **11.** 60°   **12.** 30°

13. $x = 44°$, $y = 136°$ **14.** $x = 75°$, $y = 105°$, $z = 75°$ **15.** $x = 60°$, $y = 60°$
16. $x = 68°$, $y = 112°$ **17.** 70°   **18.** $x = 80°$, $y = 75°$
19. $a = 95°$, $b = 115°$ **20.** $a = 60°$, $b = 50°$, $c = 70°$
21. 78°   **22.** $x = 60°$ **23.** $y = 45°$ **24.** $x = 75°$, $y = 65°$

Exercise 2   page 133

1. 70°   **2.** 73°   **3.** 55°   **4.** 37°
5. 23°   **6.** 74°   **7.** 66°   **8.** 40°
9. 38°   **10.** 48°   **11.** 112°   **12.** 62°
13. $a = 110°$, $b = 55°$ **14.** 23°   **15.** 34°   **16.** 39°
17. $x = 60°$, $y = 48°$ **18.** $a = 65°$, $b = 40°$ **19.** $c = 67°$, $d = 54°$ **20.** $a = 60°$, $b = 40°$
21. 108°   **22.** 50°   **23.** 76°   **24.** 270°
25. 60°   **26.** $a = 45°$, $b = 67\frac{1}{2}°$, $c = 45°$

Exercise 3   page 135

1. 57°   **2.** 49°   **3.** $c = 37°$, $d = 50°$ **4.** $x = 90°$, $y = 33°$
5. $e = 44°$, $f = 52°$ **6.** $g = 90°$, $h = 34°$ **7.** 30°   **8.** 18°
9. $m = 45°$, $n = 90°$ **10.** $x = 48°$, $y = 42°$ **11.** (a) 54°   (b) 51°   (c) 90°

Exercise 4   page 135

1. 19°   **2.** 57°   **3.** $a = 55°$, $b = 49°$ **4.** $c = 35°$, $d = 59°$ **5.** $x = 26°$, $y = 43°$
6. $m = 63°$, $n = 46°$ **7.** $a = 30°$, $c = 45°$ **8.** $x = 18°$, $y = 90°$ **9.** $a = 50°$, $y = 18°$
10. $e = 61°$, $y = 22\frac{1}{2}°$ **11.** $a = 70°$, $b = 55°$ **12.** $x = 80°$, $y = 10°$ **13.** $a = 60°$, $b = 30°$

Exercise 5   page 137

1. 68°   **2.** 40°   **3.** $x = 65°$, $y = 25°$ **4.** $a = 58°$, $b = 58°$
5. $a = 56°$, $b = 34°$, $c = 34°$ **6.** $a = 22°$, $b = 68°$

Exercise 6   page 138

1. (b) 4.2 cm   **2.** (b) 2.6 cm

Exercise 7   page 139

1. 38.7°   **2.** 48.6°   **3.** 31.0°   **4.** 54.5°   **5.** 38.7°   **6.** 17.5°   **7.** 38.9°
8. 59.0°   **9.** 39.5°   **10.** 63.6°   **11.** 24.6°   **12.** 16.9°   **13.** 36.9°   **14.** 51.8°
15. 38.1°   **16.** 47.0°   **17.** 41.3°   **18.** 62.7°   **19.** 54.3°   **20.** 66.0°   **21.** 48.2°
22. 12.4°   **23.** 72.9°   **24.** 56.9°   **25.** 36.9°   **26.** 41.8°   **27.** 78.0°   **28.** 89.4°

Exercise 8   page 141

1. 3.01 cm   **2.** 5.35 cm   **3.** 3.13 cm   **4.** 7.00 cm   **5.** 73.1 cm   **6.** 15.4 cm
7. 5.31 cm   **8.** 7.99 cm   **9.** 11.6 cm   **10.** 11.4 cm   **11.** 961 cm   **12.** 0.894 cm
13. 46.0 cm   **14.** 34.9 cm   **15.** 9.39 cm   **16.** 8.23 cm   **17.** 35.6 cm   **18.** 80.2 cm
19. 4.86 cm   **20.** 6.98 cm

Exercise 9   page 142

1. 18.4   **2.** 9.15   **3.** 10.7   **4.** 17.1   **5.** 13.7   **6.** 126   **7.** 6.88
8. 11.8   **9.** 39.1°   **10.** 19.5°   **11.** 65.6°   **12.** 63.6°   **13.** 17.6   **14.** 11.4
15. $x = 8.39$, $y = 64.5°$ **16.** $y = 6.29$, $e = 64.5°$ **17.** 72.0   **18.** $x = 9.51$, $y = 8.24$, $z = 6.31$
19. $x = 17.8$, $y = 16.7$, $z = 14.4$ **20.** 17.8

Exercise 10   page 143

1. 8.29   **2.** 48.6°   **3.** 53.1°   **4.** 8.60   **5.** 90.0   **6.** 9.80   **7.** 6.27

8. 31.8°   **9.** 5.66   **10.** 441   **11.** 50.5°   **12.** 8.99   **13.** 14.4   **14.** 76.0°
15. 10.2   **16.** 0.460   **17.** $x = 3.50, y = 6.63$ **18.** $x = 8.83, y = 7.68$
19. 2.53   **20.** 25.4°

Exercise 11   *page 144*

1. 68.0°   **2.** 53.1°   **3.** 2.54 m   **4.** 3.65 m   **5.** 14.0 m   **6.** 19.8 m
7. 11.9 m   **8.** 20.6°   **9.** 15.1°   **10.** 56.7 m   **11.** 29.4 m   **12.** 33.4°
13. 15.3 m   **14.** 90.3 cm   **15.** 4.32 cm   **16.** 7.66 cm   **17.** 83.6°   **18.** 7.20 cm

Exercise 12   *page 145*

1. 65.5 km   **2.** 189 km   **3.** 46.9 km   **4.** 460 km   **5.** 25.7 km   **6.** 139 km
7. 13.8 cm   **8.** 37.3 m

PART 9

Revision test 1   *page 146*

1. 3p   **2.** 200 g   **3.** £8   **4.** £92   **5.** (a) 1810 s   (b) 72.4 s   **6.** 0.8 cm
7. (a) £13   (b) £148   (c) £170   **8.** (a) $5\frac{8}{9}$ (b) 6   (c) 7
9. (a) −11   (b) 23   (c) −10   (d) −20   (e) 6   (f) −14
10. (a) 3   (b) 5   (c) −6   (d) −7
11. (a) 9   (b) 11   (c) 3   (d) 7   **12.** (a) 42 cm²   (b) 36 cm²
13. (a) y-values −7, −5, −3, −1, 1, 3, 5   **14.** (d) A′(6, 3), A″(1, 2), A*(−5, −6)
15. (d) P′(1, −1), P″(−3, 3), P*(3, 1)

Revision test 2   *page 148*

1. (a) 7   (b) $\frac{1}{4}$ (c) $\frac{4}{5}$ **2.** (a) 7.21 cm   (b) 9.22 cm   (c) 7.33 cm
3. (a) $\frac{3}{8}$ (b) $\frac{5}{8}$ **4.** (a) $\frac{2}{11}$ (b) $\frac{5}{11}$ (c) $\frac{9}{11}$
5. (a) 20 s   (b) 30 km/h   (c) 12 miles   **6.** (a) 2.088   (b) 3.043
7. (a) 91.5 cm²   (b) 119 cm²   **9.** 18 square units   **10.** (a) 0.932 cm   (b) 6.25 cm

Revision test 3   *page 149*

1. (a) £0.18   (b) 11 kg   **2.** (a) 3017, 3047, 3407, 3740   (b) 0.13, 0.151, 0.301, 0.31
   (c) 0.075, 0.715, 0.75, 7.5   (d) 0.0095, 0.089, 0.09, 0.9   **3.** 10 h 30 min
4. (a) 4.1 m   (b) 6300 cm   (c) 0.48 kg   (d) 2200 m   (e) 7 cm   **5.** £10; £30; £40
6. (a) £26   (b) £3.52   (c) £0.87   (d) £0.84   **7.** £56
8. (a) 38.7°   (b) 56.3°   (c) 36.9°   (d) 34.8°
9. (a) 62.8 cm³   (b) 268 cm³   (c) 262 cm³   **10.** (a) 5   (b) $\frac{2}{3}$ (c) 4   (d) 3
11. (a) 30, 37   (b) 12, 10   (c) 7, 10   (d) 8, 4   (e) 26, 33
12. (d) (−1, 3), (1, −3), (1, 1), (3, 1)

Examination exercise 1   *page 151*

1. £25.60, £6.70, 4, £55.30   **2.** (a) back 5, bottom 6   (b) A 6, B 4, C 5   **3.** 12 km
4. (i) 9   (ii) 50   (iii) (7 × 11) − 6 = 72 − 1   **5.** 17.7 cm   **6.** (i) 6   (ii) 5
7. (i) £100   (ii) 500   (iii) £6 loss   **8.** (a) 5.74 m   (b) 53.1°   **9.** (d) 4   (e) 4
10. (a) 500 m³   (b) 13 m   **11.** (a) 5 cm, 13 cm, 13 cm, 13 cm   (b) 120 cm³
12. (i) $\frac{2}{5}$ (ii) $\frac{7}{12}$ (iii) $\frac{7}{20}$

Examination exercise 2   *page 154*

1. (a) £5.20   (b) 29 min   **2.** (a) 2 cm   (b) 8 m
3. (a) £161   (b) £536.25   (c) £193   (d) 8

4. (a) 4   (b) 19   **5.** 74 m   **6.** 28274, £79.15, £85.42, November
7. (a) 560 kg, 57 kg   (b) 50 kg   **8.** (i) 182 cm^2 (ii) 82 cm^2 (iii) 60 cm^3
10. (a) 198 cm^3 (b) 1357 mm^3 (c) 145   **12.** (i) 43 min 32 s   (ii) 1 hr 5 min 18 s
(iii) 2 hr 8 min 6 s   (v) 10:07:38

Examination exercise 3   *page 157*

1. (a) 34 m   (b) 17   **2.** £1359
3. (a) (i) 13, 49, 109   (ii) 4, 49   (iii) 13, 109   (b) (i) 27   (ii) 33   (c) 148, 193
(d) 94, 127
4. (ii) 30 km   (iv) 40°   (v) 050°   **5.** (b) (i) £990   (ii) 54°   (iii) 6.67%
6. (a) 140 min   (b) $T = 40 M + 20$ **7.** (i) 34   (ii) 9   **8.** (a) 200   (b) $\frac{4}{25}$
9. (b) (i) 94 cm^2 (ii) 376 cm^2 **10.** (i) £6.24   (ii) £15   (iii) 24p   **11.** (i) £14.17   (ii) 6
12. (b) 96° (±1°)   (c) 410 m (±10 m)

Examination exercise 4   *page 162*

1. (a) £28 600   (b) 198   (c) £143   (d) £28 314   (e) £286
2. (a) 55p   (b) 760
3. (a) (i) 804 m^2 (ii) 64   (b) (i) 105 cm^2 (ii) 21 000 cm^3
4. (a) 8 cm   (b) 0.8   (c) 12.5 cm   **5.** (a) £6.80   (b) £31.36   (c) £22.95
(d) (i) 1555   (ii) 2 h 15 min   (iii) 64 km/h   (e) (i) 1156   (ii) 9 min
6. (i) 23, 22, 13, 13, 8, 1   (ii) 1   (iii) 2.55
8. (a) 14 cm   (b) 70°   (c) ADC, CDE   (d) ABC, BCD   **9.** 9.0 cm
10. 100
11. (a) (i) 3 h 30 min   (ii) 3 h 25 min   (iii) 720 km/h   (b) (i) £225   (ii) £950
(c) (i) 240   (ii) £185
12. (a) 6 cm, 20 cm   (b) (i) 4 cm   (ii) 48 cm^2 (iii) 960 cm^3 (c) 6 cm, 8 cm, 37°

Examination exercise 5   *page 166*

1. (a) £790   (b) £4266   (c) £5056   **2.** (a) 27 m^2 (b) 123 m^2
4. (b) (i) £114   (ii) £3.80   **5.** (i) 08096   (ii) 83 km   (iii) 15
(iv) £6.60   **6.** (i) 111 m   (iii) 48 m
8. (b) (i) 9.7 cm (±0.1)   (ii) 485 m (±5 m)   (c) (i) 42° (±1°)   (ii) 122°   (iii) 302°
(d) 410 m   **9.** (a) 70 km/h   (b) 68 km   (c) 52 km/h   (d) 5 h 25 min   (e) 1910

THINK ABOUT IT   3

Project 1   *page 170*

(e) $n = 4s + 4$ Oblong lawns   (c) $n = 4w + 6$ (d) $n = 6w + 4$

Exercise A   *page 172*

1. 90 kg   **2.** £5.04; 36p; 6; £8.34   **3.** 352 miles   **4.** 1640 nautical miles   **5.** 165 nautical miles
6. 25   **7.** 55 m.p.h.   **8.** 62 km/h   **9.** $8\frac{1}{2}$ m.p.h.   **10.** (a) 148 cm   (b) 152 cm

Project 2   *page 173*

Highest finish = 170   (60 + 60 + 50)

Exercise B   *page 173*

1. 1936 cm^3 **2.** (a) £4   (b) 100 kg   (c) 98 m   **3.** 120°   **4.** 120
5. $\frac{1}{2}$ of 0.2   **6.** 7 years   **7.** 25 litres   **8.** (a) £10   (b) 35p   (c) £3.60
9. 12 h 30 min   **10.** (a) 350 km   (b) 14 litres   (c) £6.02   (d) 20 litres

Project 3   *page 174*

For five discs 35 moves are needed.

Exercise C   *page 175*

1. 120 000 000 m^3 **2.** (a) 3 h 20 min   (b) 3 h 20 min   (c) 2 h 30 min   (d) 5 h 5 min
3. (a) £222   (b) £249   (c) 5 h   **4.** 15 cm^2 **5.** 85 km/h
6. (a) 5.4 km   (b) 0.6 cm   **7.** (a) 3 cm^2 (b) 27 cm^2 (c) $A = \dfrac{C^2}{12}$
8. 16   **10.** (a) $1\frac{1}{15}$ (b) $\frac{4}{15}$ (c) $\frac{4}{15}$

Exercise D   *page 177*

1. (a) 108 000 lb   (b) 4500 lb
2. (a) (i) £496   (ii) £680   (b) (i) £646   (ii) £890   (c) £244
3. (a) 1.75   (b) 0.35   (c) 17.87   (d) 0.08   (e) 0.08   (f) 78.09
4. (a) 8.94 cm   (b) 6.71 cm   (c) 11.2 cm   (d) 6.00 cm   **5.** (a) £1.60   (b) £4.00
6. (b) 108°

Project 5   *page 178*

(a) (i) 24   (ii) 16   (iii) 30   (b) (i) 15   (ii) 28   (iii) 45
(c) (i) 17   (ii) 7   (iii) 22   (d) (i) 78   (ii) 38   (iii) 48   (iv) 58
(e) If one or both numbers are even: multiply numbers and divide by 2.
    If both numbers are odd: multiply numbers, take away one and divide by 2.

Project 6   *page 179*

One solution is:

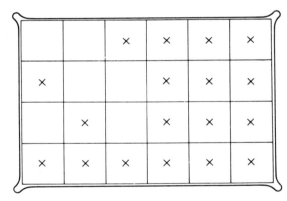